Prince George's County
Maryland
Land Records
1696-1702

Editor
Shirley Langdon Wilcox, CG

Assistant Editor
Betty Johnson McDaniel

Deed Abstractors
Records Committee
Laird C. Towle, Ph.D.
Elaine Ramsten Wells

Prince George's County
Genealogical Society, Inc.

HERITAGE BOOKS
2007

HERITAGE BOOKS

AN IMPRINT OF HERITAGE BOOKS, INC.

Books, CDs, and more—Worldwide

For our listing of thousands of titles see our website
at
www.HeritageBooks.com

Published 2007 by
HERITAGE BOOKS, INC.
Publishing Division
65 East Main Street
Westminster, Maryland 21157-5026

Other books by the author:

CD: *Prince George's County, Maryland Genealogical Society Bulletin, Volumes 1-30*
Records of the Almshouse of Prince George's County, Maryland

Library of Congress Card Catalog Number 88-124200

International Standard Book Number: 978-1-58549-580-8

FOREWORD

The decision to abstract the first volume of Prince
George's County deeds was made soon after the formal
organization of the Prince George's County Genealogical Society. Deed abstracting began in July 1971
from a microfilm copy of Deed Book A on loan from the
Maryland Hall of Records. Progress was slow as many
members were reluctant to transcribe records because
of difficulties in reading the old handwriting. One
of our out-of-state members finished the abstracting,
after which the deeds were rechecked by a local mem-
ber. The two abstractions were then compared by the
editor and the deeds were again reviewed to resolve
any discrepancies between the two copies. When interpretation of the handwritten records was difficult,
published source records on early Marylanders were
checked as an aid to correct interpretation. We
therefore hope that errors in transcribing have been
kept to a minimum. Readers interested in obtaining
photocopies of the documents abstracted in this volume
may order them from the Maryland Hall of Records,
Annapolis, MD 21404.
   In 1696 Prince George's County was created out of
land formerly belonging to Calvert and Charles Counties. Readers wishing to trace land transactions
prior to 1696 must check the deed records of Calvert
and Charles Counties.
   Aside from mention of Indian establishments, the
only Prince George's County town found in Deed Book A
is Charles Town. The land for Charles Town, called
"Mount Calvert," was taken from the northeast corner
of the 1000 acre tract called "Mount Calvert Manor,"
which had been granted to Phillip Calvert, 17 February
1658. The names Charles Town and Mount Calvert were
used interchangeably during the time period of Deed
Book A.
   Any reader who has ever worked with old documents
realizes that spelling was subject to variation as
surnames and other words were often spelled two or
three different ways within the same document. For
easy reading of this volume some of the spelling has
been changed to meet current accepted practices.
Original spellings of the names of individuals, tract
names, and geographic names have been kept. The abbre-
viation of first names took many forms in the original

documents; the original spelling of abbreviations has
been maintained, although an apostrophe has been add-
ed in some instances to denote omission of letters and
a period has been used in place of the colon found at
the end of some abbreviations.

Another peculiarity found in colonial documents is
the system of double dating. For the benefit of those
unfamiliar with the system, a brief explanation may be
helpful. Until 1752 two calendars were in use, the
Julian and Gregorian. New Year's Day on the Julian
calendar was March 25th, not January 1st as on the Gregorian calendar. When a date such as 12 February 1697/8
appears, it means the year was 1697 on the Julian calendar (the year 1698 would not begin until March 25) and
1698 on the Gregorian calendar. Sometimes a busy clerk
simply wrote "1697/" or "1697." On page 54 of this
volume there is a deed written 25 November 1700 and
shown recorded 10 February 1700. Obviously a deed can-
not be recorded before it is written. The 10 February
1700 date is a Julian calendar date which would be 10
February 1701 by the Gregorian calendar. Further and
more complete explanation of the two calendar systems
and the date of changeover can be found in books for
beginning genealogists.

The inexperienced reader should also be aware that
many terms used to designate relationships had several
different meanings during the seventeenth century. For
instance "father-in-law," in addition to today's meaning,
might be used to mean "step-father." A discussion of
such terms and their meanings may be found in genealogical textbooks.

Deed Book A contains occasional clerical pagination
errors. After page 69 are pages 60A through 69A, then
page 70 begins the correct numbering sequence again.
Page 237 is suceeded by page 286 with the intervening
numbers never used and page 293 is followed by page
293-A. All deeds in this transcription are found in
the same order as in the original deed book.

As terms for waterways may be confusing to readers,
the following explanation taken from <u>Colonial Piscataway
in Maryland</u>, by Katherine A. Kellock, has been included.

> "In the 18th century "a creeke" was a bay
> or cove; a small stream emptying into it
> was "the main fresh" or "the runne"; and
> the tributaries were "branches."

As editor I would like to thank all the members of the Prince George's County Genealogical Society who helped in the compilation of this volume. Special acknowledgements are due Elaine Ramsten Wells and Laird C. Towle, Ph. D., who did the bulk of the abstracting and Betty Johnson McDaniel who was assistant editor. The members of our Society hope that this volume will prove helpful to those genealogists and historians searching the early records of Prince George's County, Maryland.

Shirley Langdon Wilcox, C. G.
Editor

ABBREVIATIONS

Ackn'd	Acknowledged
Capt.	Captain
Co.	County
Col.	Colonel
Esq.	Esquire
etc.	et cetera
gent.	gentleman
Jr., Jun., Jun'r, Junr.	Junior
lbs.	pounds
Maj.	Major
Mt.	Mount
p.	page
P. G.	Prince George's
sic	Indicates quotation is literal and questionable or incorrect.
St.	Saint
Sr., Senr.	Senior
Wit.	Witness
Vol.	Volume

Indenture, 4 July 1696
From: MARY YATES of Anne Arundel Co., widow
To: CHARLES WILLIAMS of P. G. Co., planter
Price: 7000 lbs. tobacco
Property: A 200 acre tract called "Huckleberry
Patch" on the west side of western branch of the
Patuxent River in P. G. Co., being part of a tract
called "Vale of Benjamin," bounded by land laid
out for MARINE DEVALL called "Poplar Ridge."
Signature: MARY YATES (mark)
Wit.: JOHN GALE, MAREN DEVALL, CHARLES TRACEY
Ackn'd: MARY YATES, 4 July 1696
Recorded: 29 August 1696, Vol. A, p. 1

Indenture, 26 August 1696
From: JOHN SCOTT
To: NINIAN BEALL
Price: 8000 lbs. tobacco
Property: A 340 acre tract called "Dunkell" in
Calvert Co., lying in the "ffreses" and in the
fork of the river (not named), being part of a
warrant for 1150 acres granted to GEORGE YATES
(also spelled YEATES), 8 December 1681. The 340
acres was patented to JOHN SCOTT by CHARLES, Lord
Baltimore, 10 August in the 8th year of his reign.
Signature: JOHN SCOTT
Wit.: WILLIAM HUTCHISON, JOHN WIGHT
Ackn'd: JOHN SCOTT, 26 August 1696
Recorded: 29 August 1696, Vol. A, p. 3

Deed of Gift, 24 September 1695
From: JOHN BROWNE of Calvert Co., planter
To: THOMAS DAVICE of Calvert Co., and HONNOR his
wife, during their natural life.
Price: Love and affection
Property: The east part of a tract called "War-
mister" as divided by a branch called Little Branch,
said land now in the tenure and occupation of

FFRANCIS BILLINGER, planter, of Calvert Co., let
to him and ELLINOR his wife, by lease for ten years;
they not to be disturbed during the term of the
lease; after the decease of THOMAS DAVIS and HONNOR
his wife, land to go to their eldest son THOMAS
DAVIS "My Godson," to him and his lawfully begotten
heirs; but if he should die without lawful issue,
then land to revert to said JOHN BROWNE or his heirs.
Signature: JOHN BROWN
Wit.: EDWARD WILLETT, ARCHABLE EDMONSON, WILLIAM
POWELL.
Ackn'd: (none)
Recorded: 29 August 1696, Vol. A, p. 4

Indenture, 10 April 1696
From: WILLIAM HUTCHISON of Charles Co., gent.
To: JOHN LOWE and GEORGE DENT of St. Mary's Co.,
carpenters.
Price: 10 shillings
Property: All the tract in Charles Co. called "The
Garden," bounded by a tract called "Brothers Joynt
Interest," land of PHILLIP LYNES called "Hopewell,"
and Oxen Run.
Signature: WILLIAM HUTCHISON
Wit. WILLIAM DENT, JOHN LANNUM (mark)
Ackn'd: (none)
Recorded: 22 September 1696, Vol. A, p. 6

Indenture, 7 September 1695
From: RICHARD EDWARDS of Calvert Co., planter
To: JOHN MILLS of Calvert Co., planter
Price: 2520 lbs. tobacco
Property: 40 acres on the west side of the north
branch of the Patuxent River in Calvert Co., all the
tract originally laid out to THOMAS LETCHWORTH,
bounding on FFENDALL'S land called "Ffendalls
Spring" now in the possession of THOMAS WILLSON,
and by land of JOHN TATE.
Signature: RICHARD EDWARDS
Wit.: JOHN CHITTAM, EDWARD WILLETT
Ackn'd: RICHARD EDWARDS and HANNAH his wife,
27 September 1695.
Recorded: 22 September 1696, Vol. A, p. 7

Indenture, 16 September 1696

From: JOHN FFORREST of P. G. Co., planter and
ELIZABETH his wife.
To: HENRY HOW and THOMAS PALMER of P. G. Co.,
planters.
Price: 8000 lbs. tobacco
Property: 225 acres, all the tract called "The
Fforrest" on the southwest side of Patuxent River
in the woods on the main road to St. Mary's bound-
ing on the east side of a small branch of Chaplico,
and on the said road; said tract was formerly sur-
veyed in Calvert Co., but now lies in St. Mary's Co.
Signature: JOHN FFORREST (mark)
Wit.: THO. GREENFIELD, WILL'M DENT
Ackn'd: JOHN FFORREST and ELIZABETH his wife, 16
September 1696.
Recoreded: 22 September 1696, Vol. A, p. 9

Indenture, 13 November 1696
From: JOHN MIRTH, son of JOHN MIRTH late of Calvert Co. (but signed the division of the said Co.
in P. G. Co.), planter.
To: JAMES GAMBLING of P. G. Co., planter
Price: 80 pounds sterling
Property: Part of "Woods Joy" on the south side
of the Patuxent River in Calvert Co., said tract
being the "remaining part of 300 acres not formerly
sold to MICH'LL FARMER"; said tract bounding on land
of HENRY POPE and PATRICK CAMELL, and on the river.
Note - CECILIUS, Lord Proprietor, granted 500 acres
in Calvert Co., otherwise P. G. Co., on the south
side of the Patuxent River to EDWARD WOOD, 25 May
1663. This tract was known as "Woods Joy." On 2
October 1669, said EDWARD WOOD conveyed 300 acres
of this tract to JOHN MIRTH. This 300 acres was
on the south side of the Patuxent River running
from HENRY POPE'S land up the river to PATRICK
CAMELL'S land.
Signature: JOHN MIRTH (mark)
Wit.: WILL. WILKINSON, AUGUS. CARLETON, WILLIAM
BARTON, JOHN WIGHTE.
Ackn'd: JOHN MIRTH, 17 November 1696
Recorded: 24 November 1696, Vol. A, p. 12

Quit Claim, 13 November 1696
From: JAMES BIGGERS of Charles Co.

To: JAMES GAMBLING of P. G. Co.
Price: A "competent sum of money"
Property: 200 acres, part of a tract called "Woods
Joy" on the south side of the Patuxent River; sold
by JOHN MIRTH of P. G. Co. to the said JAMES GAMBLIN
by deed of this date.
Signature: JAMES BIGGERS
Wit.: WILL. WILKINSON, AUGUS. CARLETON, WILL. BARTON,
JOHN WIGHTE.
Ackn'd: (none)
Recorded: (no date specified), Vol. A, p. 14

Quit Claim, 12 November 1696
From: JOHN MIRTH, son of JOHN MIRTH, late of Cal-
vert Co.
To: Capt. JAMES BIGGERS of Charles Co.
Price: A "competent sum of money"
Property: 200 acres, part of a tract called "Woods
Joy," on the south side of the Patuxent River.
Signature: JOHN MIRTH (mark)
Wit.: GEORGE JACKSON, JAMES BOULTON (mark),
WILLIAM BARTON, JOHN WIGHTE.
Ackn'd: (none)
Recorded: 24 November 1696, Vol. A, p. 15

Indenture, 31 May 1696
From: THOMAS PAGGETT of Calvert Co., otherwise
called P. G. Co., planter, and SARAH his wife.
To: PHILLIP TETTERSHOLL (TETTERSALL) of P. G. Co.,
planter.
Price: 3000 lbs. tobacco
Property: 50 acres, part of a tract near Indian-
towne Creek, now called Fransum Creek, in the pos-
session of THOMAS PAGGETT and JOSEPH GREERE, near
the land of THOMAS HATTON, gent.
Signatures: THOMAS PAGGETT and SARAH PAGGETT (mark)
Wit.: WILLIAM BARTON, JOHN WIGHTE, SARAH BARTON
Ackn'd: THOMAS PAGGETT and wife SARAH, 31 May 1696
Recorded: 24 November 1696, Vol. A, p. 16

Indenture, 20 November 1695
From: JAMES THOMSON of Shaftsbury, Dorsett Co.,
sailorman.
To: JAMES STODDART of AnneArundel Co., planter

4

Price: 65 pounds sterling
Property: All the 500 acre tract called "Yarow"
in Charles Co., on the north side of the eastern
branch of the Potomac River; bounded by land laid
out to WILLIAM THOMPSON.
Signature: JAMES THOMSON
Wit.: JOHN HONBLON MAIJOR, JOHN SNELLSON, RICHARD
CLARKE (mark), THOMAS JACKSON.
Ackn'd: (none)
Recorded: 24 November 1696, Vol. A, p. 18

Indenture, 18 November 1696
From: RANDOLPH HANSEN of Charles Co., gent.
To: JOHN FFENDALL, carpenter, and JOSHUAH MARSHALL,
planter; both of Charles Co.
Price: 100 pounds sterling
Property: RANDOLPH HANSON of Charles Co., gentle-
man, and his wife BARBARA, appointed WILLIAM HUTCHI-
SON of P. G. Co., gentleman, attorney to deliver
into the possession of JOHN FFENDALL and JOSHUAH
MARSHALL two tracts of land near an old Indian town
called Aquakeeke, on the east side of Piscattaway
River, formerly in Charles Co., now in P. G. Co.;
said FFENDALL was to have the 500 acre tract called
"Hansonton" and said MARSHALL was to have the 360
acre tract called "Charley."
Signatures: RANDOLPH HENSON (mark) and BARBARA
HENSON.
Wit.: ROBT. WADE, ROBER. GLOVER
Ackn'd: WILLIAM HUTCHISON by letter of attorney
from RANDOLPH HANSON, 24 November 1696.
Recorded: 24 November 1696, Vol. A, p. 19

Deed, 26 November 1696
From: WILLIAM HUTCHISON of P. G. Co., gent., God-
father of PETER DENT.
To: PETER DENT, son of WILLIAM and ELIZABETH DENT
of Charles Co.
Price: 5 shillings and love and affection
Property: A 1/3 part of 1571 acre tract called
"Ffriendshipp" located about 4 miles above the falls
of the Potomac River, being part of a tract in P. G.
Co., patented in joint tenancy between JOHN ADDISON,
WILLIAM DENT, and the said WILLIAM HUTCHISON.

Signature: WILLIAM HUTCHISON
Wit.: THO. GREENFIELD, RICH. MARSHAM
Ackn'd: WILLIAM HUTCHISON, (no date)
Recorded: 26 November 1696, Vol. A, p. 23

Indenture, 24 November 1696
From: JOSHUA HALL of P. G. Co., planter
To: RICHARD ISACK of P. G. Co., tailor
Price: 18,000 lbs. tobacco
Property: All the 135 acre tract called "Plumers
Pleasure" in P. G. Co. between the north branch of
Patuxent River and Collington Branch; bounding on
tracts called "Lundy," "Cuckolds Delight," and
"Mount Pleasant."
Signature: JOSHUA HALL
Wit.: THO. GREENFIELD, CHRISTOPHER TOMSON (mark),
JOHN JOYCE.
Ackn'd: MARGARET HALL, wife of JOSHUA HALL, re-
leased her dower, 24 November 1696.
Recorded: 26 November 1696, Vol. A, p. 24

Deed, 26 August 1695
From: THOMAS SMITH of Calvert Co., planter
To: THOMAS WELLS of Calvert Co., planter
Price: 90 pounds sterling
Property: A 200 acre tract called "Strife" in Cal-
vert Co., on the west side of Patuxent River in the
freshes of the river, being part of a warrant for
4,000 acres; bounded by land laid out for FRANCIS
SWANTONE, EDWARD ISAACK, and THOMAS BOWDELLS. This
land was patented to Col. HENRY DARNALL, Esq., by
CHARLES,Lord Baltimore, in 1680; he sold the 200
acres to PETER BURGIS of Calvert Co., 8 January 1684;
said BURGIS then conveyed it to the said THOMAS
SMITH, 19 June 1688.
Signatures: THOMAS SMITH and MARY SMITH
Wit.: ROBERT WADE, JOHN UNDERWOOD
Ackn'd: THOMAS SMITH and MARY his wife, (no date)
Recorded: 26 January 1696, Vol. A, p. 26

Indenture, 31 January 1692
From: Col. NINIAN BEALL, High Sheriff of Calvert
Co., being attorney of BENJAMIN HADDOCK.

To: JOHN EMMET of Charles Co., carpenter
Price: 6000 lbs. tobacco
Property: All the 500 acre tract called "Seamans
Delight" in Charles Co., bounding on land formerly
taken up for RICHARD EVANS of Calvert Co.
Signature: NINIAN BEALL
Wit.: HUGH MOORE, WILL'M STONE, WILL'M HATTON
Ackn'd: NINIAN BEALL, 31 January 1692
Recorded: 26 January 1696, Vol. A, p. 28

Deed of Gift, 26 December 1694
From: SABINA BARNETT of Calvert Co., spinster
To: MARY BARNETT, "my daughter," minor
Price: Natural affection
Property: Home furnishings and kitchen ware to be
given to her at her marriage or coming of age, in
addition to what she was left by her father in his
will; mentions "my late husband THOMAS BARNETT" and
"his two only children," MARY BARNETT and LUKE BAR-
NETT; said LUKE is now joint Executor with SABINA
of the father's estate; if SABINA dies before the
children are set free under the terms of the father's
will, then SABINA wishes them to be "at the command
and under the tuition of Mr. THOMAS HALLYDAY," merchant of Calvert Co.
Signature: SABINA BARNETT
Wit.: JOHN CHITTAM, BENJ'A BERRY, JOSHUA HALL,
JOHN RAMSAY.
Ackn'd: (none)
Recorded: 26 January 1696, Vol. A, p. 30

Naturalization, [date illegible]
From: PROVINCE OF MARYLAND
To: DANIEL DANNISONE SR. and DANIEL DANNISONE JR.,
both of Calvert Co.
Price: (none)
Terms: Naturalized and entitled to enjoy all rights
and priviledges whatsoever within this Province as
any natural born subject.
Signature: HENRY JOWLES
Wit.: (none)
Recorded: 26 January 1696, Vol. A, p. 31

Indenture, 5 March 1694
From: THOMAS BROOKE of Calvert Co., Esq.
To: ROBERT ORME of Anne Arundel Co., planter
Price: 8000 lbs. tobacco
Property: 200 acres, part of the tract called
"Brooke Ffields" on Brooks Creek; bounded by Brooks
Creek and the Indian path, and a branch of Brooks
Creek.
Signature: THO. BROOKE
Wit.: RICHARD MARSHAM, JOHN ROADE
Ackn'd: THOMAS BROOKE, 5 March 1694/5
Recorded: 26 January 1696, Vol. A, p. 32

Indenture, 20 September 1696
From: LUKE ROAD, late of Anne Arundel Co., now of
Baltimore Co., planter.
To: MORDICAI MOORE of Anne Arundel Co., merchant
Price: 90 pounds sterling
Property: All the 300 acre tract called "Aaron"
formerly in Charles Co., now in P. G. Co., and now
occupied by said MOORE: near Annacostin Ffort;
bounded by land of LUKE GREEN and a ridge between
Oxon and the eastern branch; 300 acres according
to the certificate of survey returned to the land
office in St. Mary's City, 17 March 1687.
Signature: LUKE ROAD
Wit.: GEORGE BRAN, MORITON [JOHN MERITON], GEORGE
BRENT, JUN'R.
Ackn'd: LUKE ROAD, 18 February 1696/7
Recorded: 20 February 1696/7, Vol. A, p. 35

Indenture, 25 August 1696
From: HUGH RILEY of P. G. Co., carpenter
To: GEORGE COOPE of Anne Arundel Co.
Price: 2500 lbs. tobacco
Property: 50 acres, being part of two tracts in
P. G. Co., called "Rileys Ffolley" and "Hughs
Labour," lying on the east side of Collington
Branch.
Signature: HUGH RILEY
Wit.: JOSIAS TOWGOOD, THO. STAFFORD
Ackn'd: HUGH RILEY, 26 August 1696
Recorded: 23 March 1696/7, Vol. A, p. 38

Indenture, 24 March 1696
From: MARY YATE of Anne Arundel Co., widow
To: SAMUEL MAGRUDER of P. G. Co., planter
Price: 38 pounds sterling and 12 shillings
Property: A 192 acre tract called "Turkey Cock
Branch" in P. G. Co. on the western branch of the
Patuxent River; bounding on land of MERREN (also
spelled MARREEN) DEVALL and CHARLES WILLIAMS; be-
ing part of a tract called "The Vale of Benjamin."
Signature: MARY YATE
Wit.: JOHN SPRIGG, ALLEXANDER MAGRUDER (mark),
JOHN SUMMERS.
Ackn'd: MARY YATE, 24 March 1696
Recorded: 24 March 1696/7, Vol. A, p. 40

Indenture, 19 March 1696
From: Col. HENRY DARNALL of P. G. Co., Esq.
To: HENRY CULVER of P. G. Co., planter
Price: 12,000 lbs. tobacco
Property: A 118 acre tract in P. G. Co. called
"Woodbridge" bounded by land laid out to THOMAS
HYDE, Maj. FFITZHERBERT, and Mr. ROGER BROOKE.
This land was part of a warrant for 800 acres
granted to Col. HENRY DARNALL, 21 July 1684; he
conveyed the land to GUY FFINCH, late of Calvert
Co., who died before taking possession of the land;
REBECCA FFINCH, wife of said GUY FFINCH conveyed
the land to Col. DARNALL.
Signature: HENRY DARNALL
Wit.: CHARLES CARROLL, THOMAS ADDISON
Ackn'd: HENRY DARNALL, 21 March 1696/7
Recorded: 24 March 1696/7, Vol. A, p. 43

Deed of Gift, 4 November 1696
From: MARGERY GARDINER of St. Mary's Co., widow
To: WILLIAM WITTAM
Price: Several good causes
Property: One-half of a 200 acre tract called
"Margry" on the west side of Patuxent River in the
woods; bounded by land of ALLEXANDER MAGRUDER; orig-
inally patented in 1695.
Signature: MARGERY GARDIONER (mark)
Wit.: ROBERT STORTAN, WILLIAM DAVES
Ackn'd: (none)

Recorded: 24 March 1696/7, Vol. A, p. 44

Indenture, 22 October 1696
From: WILLIAM TURNAR of Calvert Co., gent.
To: IGNATIUS CRAYCROFT of P. G. Co., gent.
Price: 150 pounds sterling
Property: A 200 acre tract called "Acquascat" on
the west side of Patuxent River; bounding on land
of ROBERT BROOKE, Esq., and two branches called
Canadoyes and Cornelius. This tract was conveyed
by ALLEXANDER WATTS, planter, to JAMES BERRY, 10
July 1654, then to WILLIAM and NEHMIAH BERRY, from
them to JOHN GREAR, from his heirs to JOHN GALWITH
and from him and JANE his wife to the said WILLIAM
TURNAR.
Signatures: WM. TURNER and JOYCE TURNER (mark)
Wit.: PHILLIP LYNES, GEORGE MASON, JOHN CRAYCROFT,
JAMES CRANFORD.
Ackn'd: WILLIAM TURNER, 22 October 1696
Recorded: 24 March 1696/7, Vol. A, p. 44

Indenture, 30 May 1696
From: THOMAS PAGGETT of Calvert Co., otherwise
called P. G. Co., planter, and SARAH his wife.
To: JOSEPH GREERE of P. G. Co., planter
Price: (none)
Property: Western half (152 acres) of an unnamed
400 acre tract near a creek formerly called Indian-
town Creek; near land of THOMAS HATTON, gent., Secre-
tary of this Province. This 400 acre tract was orig-
inally patented to THOMAS PAGGETT and JOSEPH GREERE,
10 January 1695, and was surveyed 17 August 1653.
Signatures: THOMAS PAGGETT and SARAH PAGGETT (mark)
Wit.: WILLIAM BARTON, JOHN WIGHTE, SARAH BARTON
Ackn'd: THOMAS PAGGETT and wife SARAH, 30 May 1696
Recorded: 24 March 1696/7, Vol. A, p. 47

Indenture, 20 October 1696
From: NINEAN BEALL of Calvert Co., gent.
To: ANTHONY SMITH of Anne Arundel Co., planter
Price: 6000 lbs. tobacco
Property: All the 140 acre tract called "Smiths
Purchase" in the freshes of Patuxent River and in

10

the fork of said river; formerly laid out for JOHN
SCOTT.
Signatures: NINIAN BEALL and RUTH BEALL (mark)
Wit.: DAVID SMALL, THO. LARKIN
Ackn'd: NINIAN BEALL and RUTH his wife, 20 Dec.(?)
1696.
Recorded: 24 June 1697, Vol. A, p. 50

Indenture, 23 June 1697
From: JAMES MOORE of P. G. Co., carpenter
To: WILLIAM MOORE of P. G. Co.
Price: 1818 lbs. tobacco
Property: All the 80 acre tract in P. G. Co. called "Beales Hunting Quarter" in the freshes and in
the fork of the western branch of the Patuxent River
and on the southwest side of Collington Branch; ad-
joining land of JOHN DEMALL, Capt. BROCK, and Capt.
PERRY'S land called "Chelsey"; subject to the con-
dition that MARY FFALKNER, formerly called MARY
MOORE, being the natural mother of the said WILLIAM
MOORE, shall have possession and use of the land
during her natural life; this land was part of a 300
acre tract patented to JAMES MOORE, 1 July 1682.
Signature: JAMES MOORE
Wit.: ROBERT WADE, THOMAS SPRIGG JR.
Ackn'd: JAMES MOORE and MARY MOORE his wife, 24
June 1697.
Recorded: 24 June 1697, Vol. A, p. 52

99 Year Lease, 14 May 1697
From: NINIAN BEALL now of P. G. Co., but of Calvert
Co., before the division of the Co., gent., but for-
merly called planter.
To: JAMES STODDARD of P. G. Co., tailor
Price: 9025 lbs. tobacco and an annual rental of
one grain of Indian Corn.
Property: All the 300 acre tract in P. G. Co., for-
merly in Calvert Co., called "Bacon Hall" on the
west side of the western branch of Patuxent River;
adjoining land of BAKERS BROOKS, Esq., called "Brooke
Grove," land of PETER JOY, land laid out for THOMAS
TRUEMAN, Esq., land of JOHN BEGGER called "Mussell
Shell," and land laid out for Maj. THOMAS BROOKE
called "Grove Landing"; originally granted to NINIAN
BEALL, 1 May 1672.

Signature: NINIAN BEALL
Wit.: JOHN BATE, WILL'M HOLLYDAY
Ackn'd: NINIAN BEALL, 14 May 1697
Recorded: 24 June 1697, Vol. A, p. 54

Division, 30 May 1696
From: JOSEPH GREER of Calvert Co., otherwise called P. G. Co., planter, and SARAH his wife.
To: THOMAS PAGGETT of P. G. Co., planter
Price: (none)
Property: THOMAS PAGGETT was to have the eastern
half, and JOSEPH GREER the western half (about 152
acres) of a 400 acre tract granted to them jointly,
10 January 1695; said tract is near a brook formerly called Indiantowne Creeke, now called Transum
Creeke, near land of THOMAS HATTON, gent., and Secretary of the Province; "see certificate of survey
dated 17 August 1653."
Signatures: JOSEPH GREER (mark), and SARAH GREER
(her mark).
Wit.: WM. BARTON, JNO. WIGHT, SARAH BARTON
Ackn'd: JOSEPH GREER and SARAH his wife, 30 May
1696.
Recorded: 24 June 1697, Vol. A, p. 58

Indenture, 30 April 1697
From: WILLIAM BARTON of P. G. Co., gent.
To: THOMAS GIBBENS of P. G. Co., planter
Price: 2000 lbs. tobacco
Property: Part of a 100 acre tract in Calvert Co.,
now P. G. Co., called "Bartons Hope" on Zaniah [Zekiah]
Branch.
Signature: WILL'M BARTON
Wit.: THO. BROOKE, JNO. WIGHT, MARY SMITH (mark)
Ackn'd: WILLIAM BARTON and SARAH his wife, 30
April 1697.
Recorded: 24 June 1697, Vol. A, p. 60

Indenture, 22 February 1696
From: IGNATIUS WHEELER of Charles Co., and FFRANCIS
his wife.
To: THOMAS BOWLING of Charles Co.
Price: Love and affection
Property: All the tract of 299 acres in P. G. Co.

at Piscataway called "Indian Field," as described
in the patent.
Signatures: IGNATIUS WHEELER and FRANCIS WHEELER
(her mark).
Wit.: MATHEW BARNES (mark), LOCKLEN MUNDONE (mark)
Ackn'd: IGNATIUS WHEELER and FRANCIS his wife,
(date unspecified).
Recorded: 24 June 1697, Vol. A, p. 63

Indenture, 23 June 1696
From: HUGH RILY of P. G. Co., carpenter
To: NATHANIEL BROTHERS of P. G. Co., planter
Price: 10 pounds sterling
Property: Part of a tract called "The Begining,"
(acreage not specified), on the Patuxent River and
Collington Branch, bounding on a tract called "Scotts
Lott," and on Mr. THOMAS HOLLYDAY'S land called
"Upper Getting."
Signature: HUGH RILEY
Wit.: EDWARD WILLETT, THO. BEDGEET
Ackn'd: (none)
Recorded: 24 June 1697, Vol. A, p. 64

99 Year Lease, 24 July 169[7]
From: WILLIAM GROOME of Charlestown, P. G. Co.,
innholder, and MARY his wife; eldest son of WILLIAM
GROOME, late of Calvert Co., gent., deceased.
To: THOMAS EMMS of the City of London, mariner,
and DAVID SMALL of P. G. Co., merchant.
Price: 12,000 lbs. tobacco
Property: 163 acre portion of the tract called
"Mount Calvert" on Calverts Branch on the west side
of Patuxent River in the freshes near the dividing
of the river; bounding on land of JOHN DAVIS, CHRIS-
TOPHER BEANES, and CHARLES TRACYS, and on the road
that goes to the ferry. This was part of a 1000
acre tract granted to PHILLIP CALVERT of St. Mary's
Co., Esq., 17 February 1658, and which was conveyed
by him to WILLIAM GROOME of Calvert Co., gent., 10
April 1660. The tract was bequeathed by him to his
eldest son WILLIAM GROOME on condition that he give
500 acres to his younger brother RICHARD GROOME.
(Reference is also made to a lot leased by the said
WILLIAM GROOME JR. and his wife MARY to JOSIAS TWO-
GOOD for 99 years; date of lease unspecified.)

13

Signatures: WM. GROOME and MARY GROOME
Wit.: WM. BARTON, JNO. WIGHT, JONN'N WILLSONE,
JOSH. CECELL.
Ackn'd: WILLIAM GROOME and wife MARY, 24 July 1697
Recorded: 24 August 1697, Vol. A, p. 65

11 Year Lease, 1 August 1694
From: EDWARD TURNER of Charles Co.
To: GILBERT MASH of Charles Co.
Price: Divers causes and considerations
Property: A 400 acre tract called "Batchellors
Harbour" on Broad Creek on the east side of Potomac
River, being a farm where said TURNER now lives,
having a 15 foot dwelling house and a 10 foot hen
house.
Signatures: EDWARD TURNER and GILBERT MASH (mark)
Wit.: THOMAS PERSONE (mark), JNO. WEST, JAMES
COMPTEN.
Ackn'd: (none)
Recorded: 24 August 1697, Vol. A, p. 69

Indenture, 26 June 1697
From: GEO. AITHY of P. G. Co., planter, and SARAH
his wife.
To: WILLIAM ELLIOT of P. G. Co., planter
Price: 6800 lbs. tobacco
Property: All the 220 acre tract called "St. Johns"
in P. G. Co., formerly in Charles Co., adjoining a
tract called "Maddozes Fooly" ["Madducks Folly"].
Signature: GEORGE ATHEY (mark)
Wit.: ROB'T MIDDLETON, WILLIAM CLARKSON, THOMAS
ADDISON.
Ackn'd: GEORGE AITHEY and wife SARAH, 26 June 1697
Recorded: 24 August 1697, Vol. A, p. 60A

Indenture, 5 September 1697
From: JOHN BOYDE of P. G. Co.
To: JOHN MOBBERLY of Anne Arundel Co.
Price: 7800 lbs. tobacco
Property: All the 127 acre tract called "Amptill
Grainge" on Patuxent River in P. G. Co., bounding
on a branch of the Patuxent and a tract called
"Essington."
Signature: JOHN BOYDE (mark)

Wit.: THO'S EDMUNDSON, WILLIAM BARTON, ROBERT WADE
Ackn'd: JOHN BOYDE and wife MARY, 29 September 1697
Recorded: 29 September 1697, Vol. A, p. 62A

Petition and Deed of Gift, 10 June 1693
Between: Capt. RICHARD BRIGHTWELL and Vestry of
St. Paul.
Price: (none)
Petition: At a meeting held at Mount Calvert by the
Vestry of St. Paul, 3 June 1693, it was decided that
as the lower part of the Parish was too remote from
the church, the minister would attend every third
Sabbath at the home of Capt. BRIGHTWELL, beginning
11 June 1693. As the land near BRIGHTWELL'S plan-
tation was most fit for a chapel, the Vestry re-
quested that BRIGHTWELL grant land and timber for
that purpose. Confirmation was to take place at St.
Pauls Church in Charlestowne the first Saturday of
July [1693].
Deed of Gift: 1 July 1693, Capt. RICHARD BRIGHTWELL
granted 2 or 3 acres of land and timber for a chapel.
Signature: THO. GREENFIELD, for the Vestry
Wit.: THO. GREENFIELD, THO. HOLLYDAY, RICH. CHARLETT
Ackn'd: (none)
Recorded: 29 September 1697, Vol. A, p. 63A

Indenture, 20 April 1694
From: Col. NINIAN BEALL of Calvert Co.
To: Mr. RICHARD MARSHAM of Calvert Co.
Price: 300 pounds sterling
Property: All the 3800 acre tract called "Darnalls
Grove" on the west side of Patuxent River in the
freshes and on the west side of Collington Branch;
this 3800 acre tract in Calvert Co. was originally
granted to NINIAN BEALL, 28 June 1683.
Signature: NINIAN BEALL
Wit.: THOMAS GREENFIELD, TIM. MOHALL (mark)
Ackn'd: Col. NINIAN BEALL and RUTH his wife, 20
April 1694.
Recorded: 29 September 1697, Vol. A, p. 64A

Indenture and Release, 28 April 1697
From: WALTER BIGGER of Calvert Co., gent., son of
JOHN BIGGER of Patuxent River.

15

To: WILLIAM SELBY of P. G. Co.
Price: 100 pounds sterling
Property: All the remaining 350 acres of a tract
called "To Good" on the west side of Patuxent River;
bounded by land formerly laid out for Mr. CHRISTOPHER
ROUSBY called "Croome," by land of ROBERT RIGLEY
called "Timberly" and "Generals Gift." This was
part of a 450 acre tract in Calvert Co., now P. G.
Co., granted to JOHN BIGGER, 1 August 1672, and by
him bequeathed to WALTER BIGGER in a will dated 12
November 1675; 100 acres of the tract had been con-
veyed to JONATHAN PRATER; JOHN BIGGER, eldest son of
JOHN BIGGER, late of said Co., released all his right
and claim to the said 350 acres to the said WILLIAM
SELBY with witnesses ROB'T SKINNER, WILLIAM HEAD, and
WILLIAM BARTON. JAMES BIGGER, second son of JOHN BIG-
GER, late of Calvert Co., likewise released all his
right and claim to this lot with witnesses JOHN MURTH
(mark), and WILLIAM BARTON.
Signature: WALTER BIGGER
Wit.: NINIAN BEALL, E. BATSON, SARAH BARTON
Ackn'd: WALTER BIGGER, 28 April 1697
Recorded: 23 November 1697, Vol. A, p. 68A

Indenture, 23 November 1697
From: NINIAN BEALL of P. G. Co., gent.
To: RICHARD MARSHAM of P. G. Co., gent.
Price: 205 pounds sterling
Property: All the 400 acre tract called "Mount
Pleasant" in Calvert Co., now in P. G. Co., on the
west side of Patuxent River in the freshes of the
northern branch. This tract was originally patented
to JOHN POTTS of Calvert Co., planter, 21 October
1667, and was conveyed by him to THOMAS EYRE of
North'ton Co., Virginia, and JANE his wife, she be-
ing daughter and heir of Mr. JOHN SEVERNE. THOMAS
and JANE EYRE conveyed the tract by deed dated 29
August 1680, to NINIAN BEALL.
Signature: NINIAN BEALL
Wit.: JOHN HAWKINS, SAM'LL MAGRUDER
Ackn'd: NINIAN BEALL and RUTH his wife (mark),
23 November 1697.
Recorded: 27 November 1697, Vol. A, p. 72

Indenture, 24 November 1697

From: JOHN BOYD of P. G. Co., planter, and MARY
his wife.
To: ROGER BROOKE, JR., of Calvert Co., planter
Price: Valuable considerations
Property: Two tracts: 1) a 125 acre tract called
"Concord" in P. G. Co. on the west side of Patuxent
River in the freshes of the river as originally
granted to RICHARD BROCKDEN, said lot being bounded
by land of ROBERT ANDERSON called "Cattail Meadows"
by land of JOHN LEWELLING, and by Collington Branch;
2) a 204 acre tract being part of "Ryleys Lott" as
formerly granted to HEW RYLEY, formerly in Calvert
Co., but now in P. G. Co., on the north side of Col-
lington Branch being bounded by a part of this tract
belonging to THOMAS PINGLE, by land of ROBERT TYLER,
by Collington Branch, by land surveyed for one JOHN
LEWELLIN, and by "Concord."
Signatures: JOHN BOYDE (mark) and MARY BOYDE (mark)
Wit.: CLEBURNE LOMAX, ROBERT WADE
Ackn'd: JOHN BOYDE and MARY his wife, 24 November
1697.
Recorded: 24 November 1697, Vol. A, p. 76

Indenture, 24 November 1697
From: ROGER BROOKE, JR. of Calvert Co., gent.
To: JOHN BOYDE of P. G. Co.
Price: 15,000 lbs. tobacco and two lots, "Reighleys
Lott" and "Concord" as made over by said JOHN BOYD
to said ROGER BROOKE by deed equal date to these
presents [see above deed for descriptions of tracts].
Property: All the 350 acre tract called "Amptill
Grange" in Calvert Co. on the west side of the north
fork of Patuxent River, bounding on the river and a
tract called "Essenten" laid out for DEMETRIUS CART-
WRIGHT.
Signature: ROGER BROOKE JUN.
Wit.: CLEBORNE LOMAX, ROBERT WADE
Ackn'd: ROGER BROOKE, 24 November 1697
Recorded: 24 November 1697, Vol. A, p. 78

Quit Claim, 16 October 1697
From: HESTER BALL, widow and relict of MICHAELL
BALL, late of Calvert Co., deceased, planter.
To: EDWARD BALL of Calvert Co., planter
Price: 1600 lbs. tobacco annually during the natural

life of said HESTER BALL, payable on the 10th of
November each year.
Property: All right to the land and chattels left
by said MICHAELL BALL, deceased.
Signature: HESTER BALL (mark)
Wit.: JOHN SMITH, JOSH. CECELL
Ackn'd: (none)
Recorded: 24 November 1697, Vol. A, p. 80

Indenture, 10 December 1697
From: THOMAS TANEY of Charles Co., gent., and
JANES [sic] his wife.
To: JOHN BIGGERS; in behalf of EDWARD TRUEMAN, the
son-in-law of THOMAS TANEY, and son of HENRY TRUE-
MAN, late of Calvert Co., deceased, gent.
Price: Love and affection
Property: Two tracts: 1) part of a tract patented
to EDWARD WOOD called "Woods Joy" on the west side
of Patuxent River in P. G. Co., bounding on the
river, 180 acres; 2) and an adjoining tract called
"Timber Neck," bounding on land of IGNATIUS CREY-
CROFT, 250 acres. Said land to go to EDWARD TRUE-
MAN or his lawfully begotten heirs, but if he has
none and does not reach age 21 years, then the land
is to go to THOMAS TRUEMAN, youngest son of HENRY
TRUEMAN.
Signatures: THO. TANEY and JANE TANEY (mark)
Wit.: JOHN WIGHT, JOHN SMITH
Ackn'd: THOMAS TANEY and JANE his wife (mark), 13
December 1697.
Recorded: 25 January 1697/8, Vol. A, p. 81

Indenture, 27 September 1697
From: NICHOLAS SEWALL of St. Mary's Co., Esq.
To: THOMAS BROOKES of P. G. Co., Esq.
Price: 2000 lbs. tobacco and 200 pounds sterling
Property: Part of a tract called "Brookfield" on
the south side of Patuxent River, bounding on land
of GEORGE COLLINS. THOMAS BROOKES, late of Calvert
Co., Esq., deceased, owned a 2530 acre tract called
"Brookfield" on the south side of Patuxent River in
Calvert Co. which he bequeathed in a will dated 25
October 1676 to his eldest son THOMAS BROOKS and to
his second son ROBERT BROOKS. The latter sold his
portion through his attorney, Col. HENRY DARNALL,
by deed dated 6 January 1686 to NICHOLAS SEWALL.
Signature: NICHOLAS SEWALL

Wit.: IGNATIAS CRAYCROFT, WILLIAM BARTON, JOHN
WIGHT.
Ackn'd: NICHOLAS SEWALL and SUSANNA his wife,
27 September 1697.
Recorded: 25 January 1697/8, Vol. A, p. 83

Indenture, 13 September 1697
From: ROBERT BROOKE of P. G. Co., gent.
To: THOMAS BROOKE of P. G. Co., gent., his brother
Price: 23 pounds sterling and 7 shillings
Property: Two tracts: 1) a 129 acre tract called
"Wedge" on the west side of Patuxent River, bound-
ing on land laid out for GEORGE COLLINS called
"Twiver" on "Brookfield," and on the river; 2) all
the 33 acre tract called "Croscloth" on the west
side of Patuxent River; bounding on "Hargrove" and
on "Brookfield." Both tracts were formerly in Cal-
vert Co., but now in P. G. Co. They were original-
ly granted to Maj. THOMAS BROOKS, father of the said
THOMAS BROOKS and ROBERT BROOKS.
Signature: ROBERT BROOKE
Wit.: CLEMENT HILL JR., PHILLIP DARNALL, CLEMENT
BROOKE.
Ackn'd: ROBERT BROOKE, 13 September 1697
Recorded: 25 January 1697/8, Vol. A, p. 86

Indenture, 9 October 1697
From: JOHN GARDNER of P. G. Co., planter
To: THOMAS LAMAR of P. G. Co., planter
Price: 110 pounds sterling
Property: All the 200 acre tract called "Batchelers
Hope," and the plantation thereon on the eastern part
of a greater tract originally granted to NINIAN BEALL
called "Majors Lott" in P. G. Co., but formerly in
Calvert Co., on the west branch of the west side of
the Patuxent River in the freshes, bounded by land of
JAMES MULLIKINS, and by land laid out for Maj. SEWALL
and JOHN DARNALL.
Signature: JOHN GARDINERS
Wit.: JOHN BOYDE (mark), THO'S EDMUDSON, JOHN
BROYN (mark).
Ackn'd: JOHN GARDNER, 9 October 1697
Recorded: 25 January 1697/8, Vol. A, p. 89

19

99 Year Lease, 22 April 1697
From: WILLIAM GROOME of P. G. Co., innholder, and
MARY his wife.
To: JOSIAS TOWGOOD of P. G. Co., gent.
Price: 800 lbs. tobacco and paying yearly one fat
capon or hen on December 25th on demand.
Property: A one acre piece of a tract called "Mount
Calvert Manor" on the west side of Patuxent River
in the freshes near the dividing of said river, in
a parcel of land commonly called Charles Town.
Signatures: WM. GROOME and MARY GROOME
Wit.: RICHARD GROOME, HUGH TRACEY (mark)
Ackn'd: MARY GROOME wife of WILLIAM GROOME, 24 June
1697.
Recorded: 25 January 1697/8, Vol. A, p. 91

99 Year Lease, 28 January 1697/8
From: JOHN DAVIS of P. G. Co., planter
To: WILLIAM STONE and JOHN MERITON
Price: 800 lbs. tobacco and annual rent of one
"year" of Indian corn due on January 1st.
Property: A 2 acre parcel in Charlestowne in P. G.
Co., adjoining land of JOSHUA CECELL, laid out by
EDWARD BATSON.
Signatures: JOHN DAVIS, WM. STONE, JOHN MERITON
Wit.: JON'A WILLSON, JAMES METHUEN
Ackn'd: (none)
Recorded: 28 January 1697/8, Vol. A, p. 93

Note and Release, 28 August 1697
From: JAMES WILLIAMS of P. G. Co., planter
To: JAMES MULLIKIN of P. G. Co., planter
Property: Said WILLIAMS gave a note for 16,000 lbs.
of tobacco to said MULLIKIN, due 10 January next,
subject to the condition that if said WILLIAMS,
by the last day of November next, makes over by
deed of gift 200 acres out of the north side of a
tract called "Chelsey," now in the possession of
said WILLIAMS, unto JAMES MULLIKIN and JANE his
wife for their natural lives, and after their decease, to their second son THOMAS and his heirs,
otherwise to their eldest son JAMES and his heirs,
otherwise to descend through the whole family of
said JAMES MULLIKIN and JANE his wife, then said
note to be void.
Signature: JAMES WILLIAMS

Wit.: EDWARD WILLETT, RICHARD CHAFFEE (mark)
JAMES MULLIKIN of P. G. Co., planter, released
JAMES WILLIAMS, son of JAMES WILLIAMS, deceased,
of P. G. Co., planter, from any claims or obligations,
he now has or ever will have against him concerning
any legacies, lands, plantations, etc., which "was
given me by my father-in-law JAMES WILLIAMS, or by
my mother MARY WILLIAMS wife of the above named JAMES
WILLIAMS, given or bequeathed to me by my mother at
or before or after marriage with the said JAMES
WILLIAMS, deceased."
Signature: JAMES MULLIKIN (mark)
Wit.: EDWARD WILLETT, RICHARD CHAFFEE (mark)
Recorded: 28 January 1697/8, Vol. A, p. 94

Indenture, 25 January 1697
From: JAMES WILLIAMS of P. G. Co., planter
To: JAMES MULLIKIN of P. G. Co., planter, and JANE
his wife during their natural lives, then to their
second son THOMAS and his lawfull heirs, otherwise
to their eldest son JAMES and his lawful heirs,
otherwise to descend through the family of said
JAMES MULLIKIN and JANE his wife.
Property: All the 200 acre tract called "James Gift"
being part of a tract called "Chesley" which is now
in the possession of the said JAMES WILLIAMS.
Signature: JAMES WILLIAMS
Wit.: WILLIAM HARBERT, JOSH. CECELL
Ackn'd: JAMES WILLIAMS, 25 January 1697/8
Recorded: 28 January 1697/8, Vol. A, p. 95

Indenture, 17 September 1697
From: CHARLES GREENE of Kings Lynn, Co. of Norff,
England, apothecary, and ELIZABETH his wife, daughter
of JAMES TRUMAN, late of Maryland, deceased.
To: THOMAS GREENFIELD, gent., Province of Maryland
Price: 140 pounds sterling
Property: About 1169 acres of land being one-third
of the following tracts inherited by ELIZABETH, the
wife of CHARLES GREENE: 1) JAMES TRUMAN bequeathed
one-third of a tract, 750 acres, called "Indian
Creeke with Addition" to his wife ANN TRUMAN, and
two-thirds to his daughters MARTHA TRUMAN, MARY
TRUMAN, and ELIZABETH TRUMAN, in equal shares. ANN
TRUMAN and her second husband ROBERT SKINNER, then

21

conveyed all their one-third part to the three daughters above, equally. 2) NATHANIEL TRUEMAN owned several tracts including a 130 acre parcel called "Truemans Hills," which he bequeathed to his three nieces, ANN TRUMAN, MARY TRUMAN, and ELIZABETH TRUMAN. 3) THOMAS TRUMAN owned several tracts including 375 acres called "Trumans Choyce Deminished," 300 acres called "Retalliation," 150 acres called "Addition," 200 acres called "Mazoonscon," 110 acres called "Barrens," 162 acres called "The Goores," 75 acres called "Newton," 28 acres called "Prevention," 100 acres called "Purchase," 400 acres called "Trumans Lott," 95 acres called "Trumans Chance," 127 acres called "Trumans Hope," 50 acres called "Wolves Den," 300 acres called "Nottingham," 500 acres called "Trumans Aquaintance," all of which he bequeathed by his will of 1685 to his nieces MARY TRUMAN, ELIZABETH TRUMAN, now the wife of the above mentioned CHARLES GREENE, and to THOMAS TRUMAN, the eldest son of the above mentioned THOMAS GREENFIELD, in equal shares.
Signatures: CHARLES GREENE, ELIZ. GREENE
Wit.: JOHN MAXEY, JOHN CRYER, JOHN LINGE
Ackn'd: CHARLES GREENE and ELIZABETH his wife in England, 17 September 1697.
Recorded: 25 June 1698, Vol. A, p. 97

Indenture, 21 March 1697
From: THOMAS GREENFIELD of P. G. Co., gent.
To: WILLIAM BAYLEY of P. G. Co., cooper
Price: 8000 lbs. tobacco
Property: Two tracts called "Quick Saile" and "Archers Pasture," totaling 150 acres, in Calvert Co., now P. G. Co., on the west side of the Patuxent River in the woods, bounding on "Taylors Rest," land owned by JONATHAN SIMMONS, and Deep Creek.
Signature: THO. GREENFIELD
Wit.: THO. BROOKE, JOHN SMITH, HENRY TUNKS
Ackn'd: THOMAS GREENFIELD and MARTHA his wife, 21 March 1697.
Recorded: 27 June 1698, Vol. A, p. 101

77 Year Lease, 21 March 1697
From: THOMAS GREENFIELD of P. G. Co., gent.
To: WILLIAM BAYLEY of P. G. Co.

Price: 2000 lbs. tobacco and annual rent of one
ear of Indian corn to be paid on December 1st each
year.
Property: All the 15 acre tract called "Taylers
Rest" on the west side of Potoson [sic, Patuxent(?)]
River in the freshes; bounding on a tract called
"Quicksaile" owned by the said GREENFIELD.
Signature: THOMAS GREENFIELD
Wit.: THOMAS BROOKE, JNO. SMITH, HENRY HUNTS
Ackn'd: (none)
Recorded: 25 June 1698, Vol. A, p. 103

Indenture, 21 March 1697
From: THOMAS GREENFIELD of P. G. Co.
To: NICHOLAS DAVIS of P. G. Co., planter
Price: 2000 lbs. tobacco
Property: All the 50 acre tract called "Compass
Hills" in P. G. Co., on the west side of Patuxent
River in the freshes in the woods, and in the branch
of Aquasco Creek; bounding on land formerly granted
to JNO. BOAGUE called "Poplar Hills."
Signature: THOMAS GREENFIELD
Wit.: THOM'S BROOKE, JNO. SMITH, HENRY TUNKS
Ackn'd: THOMAS GREENFIELD and MARTHA his wife,
21 March 1697.
Recorded: 25 June 1698, Vol. A, p. 105

Indenture, 29 June 1698
From: MARY YATE of Anne Arundel Co., widow
To: JOHN CASH of P. G. Co., planter
Price: 4000 lbs. tobacco
Property: All of a 100 acre tract in P. G. Co. ad-
joining land of CHARLES WILLIAMS.
Signature: MARY YATES
Wit.: WILLIAM BARTON, JOHN WIGHT
Ackn'd: MARY YATTE, 29 June 1698
Recorded: 29 June 1698, Vol. A, p. 106

Indenture, 7 May 1698
From: RICHARD GROOME of P. G. Co., gent., and ANN
his wife.
To: WILLIAM SELBEY of P. G. Co.
Price: 4800 lbs. tobacco
Property: The eastern half of a tract called

"Essex Lodge"; 150 acres in P. G. Co., on the west
side of the Patuxent River in the woods near Matta-
pony Creek.
Signatures: RICH'D GROOME and ANN GROOME (mark)
Wit.: JOSIAS TOWGOOD, JOHN BROWEN
Ackn'd: ANN GROOME, wife of RICHARD GROOME, 17 May
1698.
Recorded: 29 June 1698, Vol. A, p. 108

Power of Attorney, 17 December 1697
From: PHILLIP PARK of London, England, merchant
To: JOHN LEROUNT of London, England, mariner
Property: Said PARK authorized said LEROUNT to
collect from THOMAS TAWNEY (also TANNEY) and others
in Patuxent River, payment for merchandise shipped
aboard the *Richmond Pink* of London.
Wit.: EDWARD BARECROCK, BENJ'A ALLCHURCH
Recorded: 29 June 1698, Vol. A, p. 109

Indenture, 21 June 1697
From: NATHANIEL BROTHERS of Calvert Co., planter
To: CHARLES HYATT of Calvert Co., cooper
Price: 3000 lbs. tobacco
Property: Part of a tract called "Beginning" on
Patuxent River in the fork, bounding on "Scotts
Lott," Mr. THOMAS HOLYDAY'S land called "Upper Get-
ting," and Collington Branch.
Signature: NATH. BROTHERS (mark)
Wit.: EDW'D WILLETT, ALEX'R WILSON
Ackn'd: MARY, wife of NATHANIEL BROTHERS, 21 June
1697.
Recorded: 29 June 1698, Vol. A, p. 110

90 Year Lease, 29 June 1698
From: JOHN DAVIS of P. G. Co., planter
To: JOSHUA CECILL of P. G. Co.
Price: 800 lbs. tobacco and yearly rent of one
ear of Indian corn to be paid on 25 December each
year.
Property: A 2 acre parcel from the tract called
"Mount Calvert Manor," formerly leased to JOHN DAVIS
by WILLIAM GROOME, lying on the west side of the
Patuxent River near the dividing of the river in
the freshes; bounding on a tract called Charles

Towne.
Signature: JOHN DAVIS
Wit.: JOHN WIGHT, JOHN HAWKINS
Ackn'd: (none)
Recorded: 29 June 1698, Vol. A, p. 111

Indenture, 6 May 1698
From: WILLIAM ROUSBEY of London, England, merchant
To: Col. HENRY DARNALL of P. G. Co., Esq.
Price: 110 pounds sterling
Property: The 1100 acre tract called "Croome" on
the west side of Patuxent River in the freshes, on
Charles Branch; bounding on land laid out for CHARLES
BROOKS. This land was originally patented to CHRISTO-
PHER ROUSBEY, then of the Province, on 1 September
1671. The land was willed by him to CHARLES BUTLER,
a natural or reputed son, but CHARLES died intestate,
underage, and without issue, so the land reverted
to Lord Baltimore who then granted the land to
WILLIAM ROUSBEY, the brother of the said CHRISTOPHER
ROUSBEY, 12 January 1692.
Signatures: WILLIAM ROUSBY, CHARLES CARROLL, RO.
CARVILE. (Said CHARLES CARROLL, Esq., and ROBERT
CARVILE, gent., both of Maryland were acting on power
granted by WILLIAM ROUSBEY at London, England, 25
December 1697.)
Wit.: THOMAS CRUNWYN, JAMES CULLEN, ROB. BENNETT
Ackn'd: By "attornies" (not named) for WILLIAM ROUSBEY,
12 May 1698.
Recorded: 29 June 1698, Vol. A, p. 112

Indenture, 28 June 1698
From: HUGH RILEY of P. G. Co.
To: SOLOMON ROTHERY of Anne Arundel Co., planter
Price: 39 pounds sterling
Property: 130 acres in P. G. Co. on Collington
Branch being a tract called "Second Lott" which was
deducted from "The Beginning" and "Rileys Folly";
bounding on land laid out for JOHN TURNER, and on
JOHN DEMALL'S tract called "Something."
Signature: HUGH RYLEY
Wit.: JOHN E. TURNER, JOSH. CECELL
Ackn'd: HUGH RILEY and MARY his wife, 28 June 1698
Recorded: 29 June 1698, Vol. A, p. 115

25

Indenture, 28 June 1698
From: HUGH RILEY of P. G. Co.
To: JOHN TURNER of P. G. Co., planter
Price: 59 pounds sterling and other considerations
Property: 107 acres in P. G. Co. on Collington
Branch being a tract called "The First Late" which
was deducted from a tract called "The Beginning";
bounding on "Majors Lott," and land of JOHN DEMALL
called "Something."
Signature: HUGH REALE
Wit.: SOLLO. ROTHERY, JOSH. CECILL
Ackn'd: HUGH RILEY and wife MARY, 28 June 1698
Recorded: 29 June 1698, Vol. A, p. 117

99 Year Lease, 29 June 1698
From: WILLIAM GROME (GROOME), P. G. Co., innholder
To: JOHN DEAKINS of P. G. Co., carpenter
Price: 1200 lbs. tobacco and one ear Indian corn
yearly on December 25th.
Property: 32 and 1/2 acres, part of a tract called
"Mt. Calvert Manor" on the west side of Patuxent
River in the freshes near the dividing of the river;
bounding on land of Mr. CHRISTOPHER BANES, on land
formerly leased to JNO. DAVIS by said GROOME, on
land of Capt. THOM'S EMMS and DAVID SMALL formerly
leased to them by said GROOME.
Signature: WILLIAM GROOME
Wit.: ALIX. MAGRUDER (mark), WILL. WYLIS (mark)
Ackn'd: WILLIAM GROOME and MARY his wife, 29 June
1698.
Recorded: 29 June 1698, Vol. A, p. 120

Petition and Court Proceedings Relating to Petition
(Petition not dated)
Petitioner: PHILLIP CLARKE of St. Mary's Co.
To: EDMOND ANDROSE, Governor of Virginia
     The Petitioner, PHILLIP CLARKE, in the late
revolution was admitted and sworn an attorney in
the Provincial Court and in several County Courts
in the Province and practiced in the same until 10
August last at which time he received a summons to
serve his Majesty as a Justice in the Provincial
Court. CLARKE then petitioned the Governor request-
ing that he not be discharged as an attorney in
order to become a Justice because he had served

during the late revolution and his family was dependent on his earnings as an attorney. The Governor did not grant that petition so CLARKE accepted the Justice's commission hoping to continue to act as an attorney in the County Courts. The Governor at the December Court "conceived a prejudice against ye petitioner" because CLARKE would not grant a judgement against Col. JOHN COOD contrary to law. The Governor then came to Court four days and attempted to show that CLARKE was guilty of some crime that might deserve CLARKE'S imprisonment, but the evidence was not there. On 14 December, by an order of Council, CLARKE was dismissed as a Justice and refused the right to practice law in any Court in the Province. The Governor also presented a proclamation promising a reward of 20 pounds sterling to any person who would swear that CLARKE was endeavoring to raise a rebellion in St. Mary's Co., from which grevious oppression and unheard of proceedings CLARKE humbly prays that he may be protected in the Colony of Virginia.

June Court 1698: [The Petition, summarized above, apparently fell into the hands of Maryland authorities because the following court records are included with the petition record.] The matter was brought before a grand jury consisting of HENRY TENNLY, foreman, JNO. SCOTT, ROBERT HOBBS, THOMAS WELLS, THOM'S SAMU'LS, SAM'LL GRAY, WILL'M ELDIN, JO. PEAKE, JNO. CHAIRES, BENJ'IN RICHARD, MORG'N JONES, RICH'D BENTON, JO. ODEN, HENRY ELDERSLEY, EDWARD LARRIMORE, RALPH SMITH, EDWARD RUIPOTT, JNO. JACOB, AARON RAWLINGS, JNO. SERGENT, JOHN ALFORD, and JNO. Mc C[illegible]. The grand jury read and approved a report from a committee consisting of JOHN HAMMOND, RICH'D HILL, THOM'S TASKER, WILLIAM HATTON, PHILLIP HOSKINS, and THOM'S STALEY stating that the committee members had seen a paper [perhaps the above petition] produced by FRANCIS NICHOLOSON, Esq., Governor of the Province, in what appeared to be the handwriting of PHILIP CLARKE of St. Mary's Co. which contained false, slanderous, and lying reflections on the Governor [as mentioned in the preceding Petition] which the committee proceeded to refute.

At a Provincial Court held in Annapolis, 14 December 1696, with Justices ROBERT SMITH, PHILLIP PARKE, RICH'D HILL, THOMAS TASKER, PHILLIP HOSKINS, and THOMAS STALEY present, Mr. PHILLIP CLARKE, one of the Justices, was charged with several crimes

and misdemeanors against the government and the
Governor. The grand jury issued an indictment
against PHILLIP CLARKE.
    Mr. PHILLIP CLARKE posted bond of 500 pounds
sterling with sureties ROB'T CARVILE and WILLIAM
TAYLARD, gent., posting 250 pounds sterling each to
guarantee CLARKE'S presence at the next Provincial
Court, 17 May 1697. At this Court the writings of
CLARKE were presented and read in Court. CLARKE
confessed to being the author of the writings and
he promised "dutyfull" behavior in the future. The
Governor then dropped all charges against CLARKE.
Recorded: 25 June 1698, Vol. A, p. 121

Indenture, 23 August 1698
From: MICHAELL ASSHFORTH of P. G. Co., carpenter
To: JOHN DEAKINS of P. G. Co., carpenter
Price: 4000 lbs. tobacco
Property: 100 acre part of a tract called "Sea-
mans Delight"; (location not stated).
Signature: MICH. ASHFORTH (mark)
Wit.: THO. HOLLYDAY, WILLIAM BARTON
Ackn'd: (none)
Recorded: 25 August 1698, Vol. A, p. 124

Indenture, 23 August 1698
From: NINIAN BEALL of P. G. Co., gent., acting as
attorney for BENJ'A HADDOCK of Charles Co.
To: MICHAELL ASHFORD of P. G. Co., carpenter
Price: 21,000 lbs. tobacco
Property: 500 acres; all the tract called "Hadducks
Hill" in P. G. Co. in the freshes of the Potomack
River on the north side of the eastern branch; ad-
joining land laid out for said HADDUCK called "Sea-
mans Delight."
Signature: NINIAN BEALE
Wit.: THOM'S HOLLYDAY, WILL'M BARTON
Ackn'd: NINIAN BEALL, 23 August 1698
Recorded: (no date), Vol. A, p. 126

Indenture, 23 August 1698
From: EDWARD BALL of Calvert Co., planter, brother
and heir at law of MICHAELL BALL, deceased, late of
Calvert Co., planter.

To: JOSHUA CECILL of P. G. Co.
Price: 78 pounds sterling
Property: A 100 acre tract called "Balls Good Luck"
in Calvert Co., now in P. G. Co., on the north side
of Mattapony Creek; bounded by land laid out for Mr.
ROGER BROOKE called "Brookes Point," and land laid
out for Major FITZHARBERT and THOMAS HYDE; originally
patented to MICHAEL BALL, 10 August 1683.
Signature: EDW'D BALL (mark)
Wit.: THO'S HOLLYDAY, WILL. BARTON
Ackn'd: EDWARD BALL and PRISCILLA his wife, 23 August 1698.
Recorded: 23 August 1698, Vol. A, p. 127

Mortgage, 11 November 1696
From: WILLIAM JOSEPH of St. Mary's Co., gent.
To: JOHN SMITH of P. G. Co., planter
Price: 175 pounds sterling
Property: A 1500 acre tract called "Jourdan" in
Charles Co.
Signature: JOHN SMITH
Wit.: WILLIAM HUTTCHISON, CLEBORN LOMAX
Ackn'd: WILLIAM JOSEPH of London, 19 November 1697
Recorded: 23 August 1698, Vol. A, p. 131

Bill of Sale, 27 October 1697
From: EDW'D BALL of Calvert Co., gent.
To: JOSHUA CECILL of P. G. Co.
Price: 8000 lbs. tobacco
Property: 8 head of cattle, 16 head of hogs, 7 pigs,
a bed and furniture, etc., belonging to MICHAELL
BALL deceased brother of said EDWARD BALL; all the
goods being situated on a 100 acre tract called
"Good Luck" ["Balls Good Luck"] in P. G. Co.
Signature: EDWARD BALL (mark)
Wit.: JNO. BIRD, JNO. LYONS
Ackn'd: (none)
Recorded: 23 August 1698, Vol. A, p. 132

Apprentice Indenture, 10 November 1697
From: RICHARD GROOME of St. Clemons, London, tailor,
age 26 years.
To: THOM'S ROBINSON of White Chapel, St. Mary's Co.,
"plaisterer."

Terms: Transportation to Maryland and support for
four years for RICHARD GROOME, age 26, who in the
presence of his mother, and with the consent of his
wife, SUSAN, bound himself apprentice and servant
to THOMAS ROBINSON, to serve him or his assigns in
Maryland plantations for four years after his arri-
val at the plantation.
Signature: THOMAS ROBINSON (mark)
Wit.: MARG'T GROOME [mother?], THOM. BELL
Ackn'd: RICH'D GROOME, a single man, [i.e. unin-
dentured?], 10 November 1697.
Recorded: 23 August 1698, Vol. A, p. 132

Indenture, 2 November 1697
From: RICH'D EDWARDS of P. G. Co., planter, and
HANNAH his wife.
To: PETER SCAMPER of P. G. Co., planter
Price: 50 pounds sterling
Property: 150 acres out of a 290 acre tract called
"Mount Pleasant" and another 50 acre tract called
"Good Luck," both on the west side of Patuxent River
at Fendalls Fresh. The 290 acre "Mount Pleasant"
was originally patented to THOM'S LETCHWORTH, 26
April 1658, and bounded on land formerly taken up by
JAMES BERRY, and on FENDALL'S land. It was conveyed
by him to JNO. POTTS who bequeathed it to his wife
HANNAH. The widow, HANNAH, married the above RICHARD
EDWARDS. They conveyed 100 acres of the tract to
JOHN TATE, 16 September 1691. The 100 acres bounded
on land laid out for the above JOHN POTT called
"Mount Pleasant," and on the Patuxent River. The
deed was recorded in Calvert Co. They also conveyed
40 acres of the 290 acre tract to JOHN MILLS by deed
dated 17 September 1695, and recorded in P. G. Co.
The 40 acre tract bounded on FENDALL'S land called
"Fendalls Spring," now in the possession of THOMAS
WILLSON, on land of JOHN TATE. The 50 acre "Good
Luck" was part of a tract called "Cold Spring Man-
ner" and was purchased by RICHARD EDWARDS, 17 Sep-
tember 1695, from FRANCIS COLLYER of Calvert Co.,
now of P. G. Co., gent.
Signatures: RICH'D EDWARDS, HANNAH EDWARDS
Wit.: ROB'T TYLER, THOM'S GREENFIELD, JNO. JOYCE
Ackn'd: RICH'D EDWARDS and HANNAH his wife, 2 Novem-
ber 1697.
Recorded: 28 August 1698, Vol. A, p. 133

99 Year Lease, 9 October 1698
From: WILLIAM GROOM of Charlestown, P. G. Co., inn-
holder, eldest son of WILLIAM GROOM, deceased, late
of Calvert Co., gent., and MARY his wife.
To: THOMAS EMES (or EMMES) of the City of London,
mariner, and DAVID SMALL of P. G. Co., merchant.
Price: 50 pounds sterling and annual rent of one
cock each December 25th.
Property: 250 acres, part of a tract called "Mount
Calvert," on the west side of Patuxent River in the
freshes near the dividing of the river, bounding on
Calverts Branch and land of Mr. BRADLEY, RICHARD
GROOME, CHARLES TREACY, and on the main town road.
The 1000 acre tract "Mount Calvert Manor" was orig-
inally patented to PHILLIP CALVERT of St. Mary's Co.,
17 February 1658, who conveyed all of the tract to
WILLIAM GROOME, gent., of Calvert Co., 10 April 1660.
Said GROOME then bequeathed it to his eldest son,
WILLIAM GROOME, on the condition that he deed one-
half of the tract to his younger brother, RICHARD
GROOME. Excluded from the present transaction were
those lots already taken up and built upon according
to the intent of an act of the Provincial Assembly
constituting a part of the said manor into a town
[Charles Town] and also a one acre lot leased by the
said WILLIAM and MARY GROOME to JOSIAS TOWGOOD for
99 years.
Signatures: WM. GROOME and MARY GROOME
Wit.: JOHN WEIGHT, JOHN SMITH, ANTHONY LANG
Ackn'd: WILLIAM GROOME and MARY his wife, 10 October 1698.
Recorded: 4 November 1698, Vol. A, p. 137

Indenture: 18 October 1697
From: GEORGE BURGES of Anne Arundel Co., gent.
To: JOHN GREEN of Anne Arundel Co., planter
Price: 3200 lbs. tobacco
Property: All the 200 acre tract called "Burges
Delight" on one of the branches of Patuxent River
in P. G. Co., bounding on land of DANIEL CLARK and
the branch (not named).
Signatures: GEORGE BURGES and KATHERINE BURGES
Wit.: THO. REYNOLD, MERITON
Ackn'd: GEORGE BURGES and KATHERINE his wife, 18
October 1697.
Recorded: 16 November 1698, Vol. A, p. 140

Indenture, 22 October 1695
From: ABRAHAM CLARKE of Calvert Co., planter
To: HUGH ABRAHAMS of AnneArundel Co., carpenter,
alias cooper.
Price: 5000 lbs. tobacco
Property: A 60 acre part of the tract called "Es-
sington" on the west side of Patuxent River in Cal-
vert Co. near the freshes of the river; originally
taken from "Essington" for JOHN LARKING (or LARKIN)
and ROBERT ANDERSON.
Signature: ABRAHAM CLARK
Wit.: FFRANCIS FFREEMAN, JOHN HANCE
Ackn'd: ABRAHAM CLARKE, 22 October 1695
Recorded: 28 November (year unspecified), Vol. A,
p. 143.

Indenture, 5 October 1697
From: WILLIAM BARTON of P. G. Co., gent.
To: JOHN MILLER of P. G. Co., planter
Price: 35 pounds sterling
Property: All the 130 acre tract called "Hazard" on
the west side of Patuxent River in the woods in P. G.
Co., adjoining "Brookwood."
Signature: WM. BARTON
Wit.: THO. BROOKE, JOHN WEIGHT
Ackn'd: WILLIAM BARTON and SARAH his wife, 5 October
1697.
Recorded: 29 November 1698, Vol. A, p. 146

Indenture, 19 September 1698
From: WILLIAM COLLINGS of P. G. Co., planter
To: GEORGE SPICER of Calvert Co., planter
Price: 165 pounds sterling
Property: All of three tracts totaling 809 acres
on the west side of Patuxent River in the freshes;
1) a 250 acre tract called "Mansfield" bounding on
land of ROBERT STANLEY, deceased; 2) a 309 acre tract
called "The Farme" bounding on "Mansfield" and land
of Mr. WILLIAM SELLBY; 3) a 250 acre tract called
"Collins Comfort" bounding on "Mansfield," land of
said STANLEY, the river, and Deep Creek.
Signature: WM. COLLINS (mark)
Wit.: ROB'T BRADLEY, SAM'LL MAGRUDER, ARCHIBALD ED-
MUNSON, EDWARD WILLETT.
Ackn'd: WILLIAM COLLINGS and ANN his wife, 29

September 1698.
Recorded: 30 November 1698, Vol. A, p. 148

Indenture, 28 July 1698
From: Col. NINIAN BEALL of P. G. Co., gent.
To: WILLIAM RAY of P. G. Co., planter
Price: 35 pounds sterling
Property: All the 158 acre tract called "Bred and
Cheese" in P. G. Co., bounding on land formerly sur-
veyed for Maj. THOMAS TRUMAN, on "St. Andrews," land
of Maj. SEWELL, on western branch, and on southwest
branch, originally patented to Maj. THOMAS TRUMAN.
Signature: NINIAN BEALLE
Wit.: THOM. HOLLYDAY, SAM'LL MAGRUDER, BENJA. BERRY
Ackn'd: NINIAN BEALL and RUTH his wife, 28 July 1698
Recorded: 1 December (year unspecified). Vol. A,
p. 150.

Indenture, 28 July 1698
From: Col. NINIAN BEALL of P. G. Co., gent.
To: EDWARD WILLETT of P. G. Co.
Price: 3000 lbs. tobacco
Property: Two tracts totaling 100 acres on the west
side of the western branch of Patuxent River in P. G.
Co.: 1) all of "Bealls Craft" which bounds on land
of WILLIAM SELLBY, 43 acres; 2) part of "Horse Race"
which bounds on "Bealls Craft" and on a branch call-
ed Packeletts Meddow, 57 acres.
Signature: NINIAN BEALL
Wit.: THOM. HOLLYDAY, SAM'LL MAGRUDER, BENJAMIN BERRY
Ackn'd: NINIAN BEALL and RUTH his wife, 28 July 1698
Recorded: 2 December 1698, Vol. A, p. 152

98 Year Lease, 27 August 1697
From: THOMAS EMMS of the City of London, mariner,
and DAVID SMALL of P. G. Co., merchant.
To: JAMES STODDERT of P. G. Co., tailor
Price: 800 lbs. tobacco and annual rent of one fat
hen or capon on December 25th.
Property: One acre out of a 163 acre portion of
"Mount Calvert" adjoining Col. HOLLYDAY'S land, and
Col. NINIAN BEALL'S land being part of "Mount Cal-
vert." The 1000 acre tract called "Mount Calvert
Manor" was originally patented to PHILLIP CALVERT,

Esq., 17 February 1658, it lying on the west side of
Patuxent River in the freshes near the dividing of
the river. PHILLIP CALVERT then conveyed it all to
WILLIAM GROOME of Calvert Co., gent., 10 April 1660.
Said GROOME then bequeathed the land to his eldest
son, WILLIAM GROOME, he to have his choice of one-
half the tract. The son WILLIAM GROOME,and his wife
MARY, then leased, "24 July last," 163 acres to the
said EMMS and SMALL for 99 years.
Signatures: THOMAS EMMS, DAVID SMALL
Wit.: HENRY BONNER, CHRISTOPHER BEANS, HUGH REYLEY
Ackn'd: THOMAS EMMS, 23 August 1698, and DAVID
SMALL, 27 August 1697.
Recorded: 5 December 1698, Vol. A, p. 154

Indenture, 8 December 1697
From: WILLIAM HUTCHESON of P. G. Co., and his wife
SARAH.
To: FFRANCIS GOODERWEEK JR. of Charles Co.
Price: 8000 lbs. tobacco
Property: 228 acres being the southwest half of a
tract called "Oxmontown" on Piscattaway Branch in P.
G. Co., formerly Charles Co., bounding on ROBERT
WADE'S land on Piscattaway Branch, and on "Dubling."
Signatures: WILLIAM HUCHISON and SARAH HUCHISON
Wit.: JOHN SYK (mark), FFRANCIS GOODERWEEK, SENIOR
Ackn'd: WILLIAM HUTCHESON and SARAH his wife, 8 De-
cember 1697.
Recorded: 7 November 1698, Vol. A, p. 156

Indenture, 23 January 1698
From: Col. NINIAN BEALL of P. G. Co., gent.
To: THOMAS BOX of P. G. Co., blacksmith
Price: 3000 lbs tobacco
Property: A 100 acre part of the 300 acre tract
called "Horse Race," and to be called "Smithfield"
on the west side of the western branch of Patuxent
River; bounding on Cabbin Branch and Western Branch.
Signature: NINIAN BEALL
Wit.: EDWARD WILLETT, CHRISTOPHER THOMPSON (mark)
Ackn'd: NINIAN BEALL and RUTH his wife, 23 January
1698.
Recorded: 22 March 1698, Vol. A, p. 158

Indenture, 23 February 1699
From: JOHN STANLEY of Anne Arundel Co., gent.
To: FFRANCIS SPRY of P. G. Co., mariner
Price: 20 pounds sterling
Property: All the 30 acre tract on the west side
of Patuxent River bounding on Cattail Marsh and land
of JOHN BROWNE; said land is now in the tenure and
occupation of said SPRY.
Signature: JOHN STANLEY
Wit.: EDWARD WILLETT, MERYTON
Ackn'd: JOHN STANLEY, 23 February 1698/9
Recorded: 23 March 1698/9, Vol. A, p. 160

Indenture, 2 December 1696
From: GEORGE PLOWDEN of St. Mary's Co., gent., and
MARGRETT his wife.
To: WILLIAM YOUNG of St. Mary's Co., planter, late
of the "sherifdum of Drumfrees in the parish of Wes-
ter Kirk of Eakdaile" in Scotland.
Price: 12,000 lbs. tobacco
Property: 300 acres, all of two tracts in P. G. Co.,
formerly in Calvert Co., in the freshes of Patuxent
River on the main branch of western branch; the two
tracts were called "Thorpland" and "Perry Hills,"
but are now called "St. David." The land was origi-
nally laid out to Capt. RICHARD PERRY as may appear
in PERRY'S deed to PLOWDEN dated 24 June 1684.
Signatures: GEORGE PLOWDEN, MARGRETT PLOWDEN
Wit.: SAM. PETER, ANN WIGHT
Ackn'd: MARGRETT PLOWDEN, 2 December 1696
Recorded: 15 April 1699, Vol. A, p. 161

Indenture, 29 June 1698
From: MARY YATE of Anne Arundel Co., widow
To: THOMAS JAMES of P. G. Co.
Price: 4000 lbs. tobacco
Property: 100 acre tract being part of "Vale of
Benjamin" on the west side of Patuxent River in the
freshes; bounding on land of JOHN CASH, being part
of the same tract.
Signature: MARY YATE (mark)
Wit.: WILLIAM BARTON, JOHN WIGHT, JOHN HAWKINS
Ackn'd: "made over in open court," 29 June 1698
Recorded: 13 June 1699, Vol. A, p. 162

Indenture, 10 March 1698
From: WILLIAM STONE of Charles Co., gent., and
THEADOSIA his wife.
To: JAMES BUTLER of Anne Arundel Co., planter
Price: 105 pounds sterling
Property: 445 acres in P. G. Co., formerly in
Charles Co., being one-half of the tract "Good Luck";
the tract was originally granted to ZACHARIA WADE
and LUKE GARDINER jointly; said GARDINER died and
the entire tract passed to said WADE, but WADE be-
queathed one-half the tract to the heirs of said
GARDINER with the condition that his own heir and
daughter, THEADOSIA, should have her choice of which
half of the tract she would inherit; the tract was
resurveyed for the division.
Signatures: WILL'M STONE, THEADOCIA STONE (mark)
Wit.: JOS. MANNING, FFRANCIS HARRISON, JOHN MANNING
Ackn'd: WILLIAM STONE, THEADOCIA his wife (no date)
Recorded: 14 June 1699, Vol. A, p. 163

94 Year Lease, 27 September 1698
From: JOHN DAVIS of P. G. Co., and ELIZABETH his
wife.
To: JOSHUA CECILL of P. G. Co.
Price: 15,000 lbs. tobacco
Property: 100 acre part of "Mount Calvert Manor" on
the west side of Patuxent River near the dividing
creek; except two acres formerly leased by said DAVIS
to WILLIAM STONE and JOHN MERYTON, and two acres for-
merly leased by said DAVIS to said CECILL.
Signatures: JOHN DAVIS, ELIZABETH DAVIS (mark)
Wit.: ROB. TYLER, SAMUELL MAGRUDER
Ackn'd: JOHN DAVIS and ELIZABETH his wife, 27 Sep-
tember, 1698.
Recorded: 21 June 1699, Vol. A, p. 165

Indenture, 30 March 1699
From: TEAGUE TREACY of Anne Arundel Co., cooper
To: EDWARD FENIX (also spelled PHENIX) of P. G. Co.
Price: 8000 lbs. tobacco
Property: 150 acres; all of the tract called "Cuc-
holds Poynt" in P. G. Co. on the south side of di-
viding creeks of Patuxent River; bounding on land
laid out for THOMAS TRUMAN, Esq., called "Dear
Bought," land of JEREMIAH SWILLIVAN [SULLIVAN],

land formerly laid out for CHARLES BROOKE, and by the creek.
Signature: TEAGUE TREACY (mark)
Wit.: WILL'M STONE, EDWARD WILLETT
Ackn'd: TEAGUE TREACY and MARY his wife, 27 June 1699.
Recorded: 1 June 1699, Vol. A, p. 167

Power of Attorney, 29 May 1699
From: JOHN LOWTHER of England, Commander of the *Lowther Galley*.
To: WILLIAM NORIS of Maryland, "my trusty and well beloved friend."
Terms: Authority to collect money for LOWTHER and Mr. JAMES TAYLOR & Company, merchants of London.
Signature: JOHN LOWTHER
Wit.: JAMES KEECH
Ackn'd: (none)
Recorded: 8 July 1699, Vol. A, p. 169

Deed, 1 August 1699
From: SAMUELL GRIFFETH of Calvert Co., planter
To: WILLIAM LEE of P. G. Co.
Price: 12,000 lbs. tobacco
Property: A 165 acre part of "Cold Spring Manor" on the west side of Patuxent River in the freshes; bounding on land of THOMAS WILLSON, RICHARD EDWARDS, and on Fendalls Fresh.
Signature: SAM'LL GRIFFETH
Wit.: EDWARD WILLETT, TOM. HOLLYDAY
Ackn'd: SAMUELL GRIFFETH and ELIZABETH his wife, 1 August 1699.
Recorded: 10 August 1699, Vol. A, p. 169

Deed, 23 January 1698
From: NINIAN BEALL of P. G. Co., gent.
To: JAMES BEALL of P. G. Co.
Price: 111 pounds sterling
Property: A 562 acre part of "Rovers Content," plus a 62 acre part of "Inclosure"; bounding on land of Col. HENRY DARNALL, now in the possession of Mr. CHARLES CARROLL, and on WADE'S land.
Signature: NINIAN BEALL
Wit.: EDWARD WILLETT, CHRISTOPHER THOMPSON (mark)
Ackn'd: NINIAN BEALL and wife RUTH, 23 January 1698

37

Recorded: 21 September 1699, Vol. A, p. 172

Deed, 23 January 1698
From: Col. NINIAN BEALL of P. G. Co., gent.
To: DANIELL MORIARTE of Anne Arundel Co.
Price: 28,000 lbs. tobacco
Property: All of "The Maidens Dowry" in the freshes
of Patuxent River in P. G. Co., 700 acres, bounding
on land surveyed for GEORGE LINGAN, now in the pos-
session of Col. HENRY DARNALL, and land now in the
possession of HENRY LOW.
Signature: NINIAN BEALL
Wit.: EDWARD WILLETT, CHRISTOPHER THOMPSON (mark)
Ackn'd: NINIAN BEALL and RUTH his wife, 23 January
1698.
Recorded: 21 September (year unspecified), Vol. A,
p. 173.

Deed, 28 August 1698
From: WILLIAM HARBERT of Charles Co., planter
To: FFRANCIS MARBERY of P. G. Co.
Price: 4000 lbs. tobacco
Property: 500 acres, all of "Little Eas" in P. G.
Co., formerly in Charles Co., bounding on a tract
called "Thomas his Chance," and on EDWARD PRICE'S
land called "Laset Thicket" ["Locust Thicket"].
Signature: WILLIAM HARBERT
Wit.: JOSHUA MARSHALL, FFRANCIS WHEELER, JANA.
WHEELER.
Ackn'd: WILLIAM HARBERT, 21 October 1698
Recorded: (no date), Vol. A, p. 175

Deed, 9 September 1699
From: HUGH REYLEY (also spelled RILEY, RYLY) of
P. G. Co., gent.
To: JOHN BAPTISTYLER (also spelled BAPTISTILER) of
Anne Arundel Co., planter.
Price: 30 pounds sterling
Property: A 100 acre tract called "Duchmans Imployment," being part of Reyleys Range" containing by
patent 800 acres, in P. G. Co., in the woods above
the head of Collington on the head of a branch called Horse Pen Branch of Patuxent River, "see certificate of survey"; adjoining SARAH RODRY'S land, also
part of said "Rileys Range."

Signature: HUGH RILEY
Wit.: ANTHONY DRAINE, SAMUELL FARMER
Ackn'd: HUGH RILEY and MARY his wife, 9 September 1699.
Recorded: 23 September 1699, Vol. A, p. 176

Deed, 9 September 1699
From: HUGH RYLEY of P. G. Co., gent.
To: SARAH RODERY of Anne Arundel Co., "spinster (or widdow)."
Price: 60 pounds sterling
Property: A 200 acre tract called "Widdows Purchase" in P. G. Co., in the woods at the head of Collington on the head of Horse Pen Branch of the Patuxent River, "see certificate of survey"; originally part of an 800 acre tract called "Reileys Range" patented to HUGH RILEY.
Signature: HUGH RILEY
Wit.: SAM'LL FARMER, ANTHONY DRAINE
Ackn'd: HUGH RILEY and MARY his wife, 9 September, (year unspecified).
Recorded: 24 September (year unspecified), Vol. A, p. 179.

Deed, 24 January (year unspecified)
From: JOHN CHITTAM of P. G. Co., planter
To: WILLIAM BARTON of P. G. Co., merchant
Price: 21 pounds sterling
Property: A 125 acre part of a 500 acre tract called "Exchange" now in P. G. Co., formerly in Calvert Co., on the west side of Patuxent River at the head of Deep Creek; bounding on Deep Creek, Mattapony Path (being the bounding between JOHN BOWLING and JOHN KING), and Deep Gully Branch; originally patented to JOHN BOWLING and JOHN KING.
Signature: JOHN CHITTAM
Wit.: JOSIAH WILLSON, JOSIAS TOWGOOD
Ackn'd: JOHN CHITTAM and ANN his wife, 24 January 1698.
Recorded: 25 September 1699, Vol. A, p. 182

Deed, 27 June 1699
From: JAMES MOOR of P. G. Co.
To: BENJAMIN BERRY of P. G. Co.

Price: 80 pounds sterling and 2 shillings
Property: All the 267 acre tract called "Berry
Fortune" in P. G. Co., on the west side of Patuxent
River on the north side of St. Charles Branch;
bounding on Deep Creek, St. Charles Branch, and on
land formerly owned by CHARLES BUTTLER; originally
part of a 400 acre tract called "Four Hills" that
was patented to JAMES MOOR.
Signature: JAMES MOORE
Wit.:   EDWARD WILLETT, WM. LEE
Ackn'd: JAMES MOOR and MARY his wife, 27 June 1699
Recorded: 26 September 1699, Vol. A, p. 184

Power of Attorney, 8 September 1699
From: ABELL BOND of London, England, merchant,
being bound for "Old England."
To: THOMAS SPRIGG, JR. of P. G. Co., gent., my very
good friend.
Terms: To collect accounts owing in the county and
also from GEORGE BURGES, THOMAS STOCKETT, and JOHN
JACOB, and RICH'D HARWOOD in Anne Arundel Co.
Signature: ABELL BOND
Wit.:   JN'A BOYD (mark), JOHN EDWARDS, HANN EDWARDS,
(her mark).
Proved: JOHN EDWARDS and his wife, 28 October 1699
Recorded: (day & month unspecified) 1699, Vol. A,
p. 185.

Deed, 24 November 1699
From: ROGER BROOKE of Calvert Co., gent.
To: JAMES BROOKE of P. G. Co.
Price: 5 shillings and love and affection for his son.
Property: A 1100 acre tract called "Brooks Reserve,"
and also a 250 acre tract called "Brooks Poynt," both
on the west side of Patuxent River in P. G. Co.
Signature: ROGER BROOKE
Wit.:   ROBT. BROOKE, MICH. TANEY, HENRY CULLVER (mark)
Ackn'd: (no name), 24 November 1699
Recorded: (day & month unspecified) 1699, Vol. A,
p. 185

Deed, 4 September 1699
From: Major NICHOLAS SEWELL of St. Mary's Co.
To: RICHARD HARRISON of Calvert Co., merchant
Price: 325 pounds sterling.

Property: A 1628 acre tract in P. G. Co., formerly
in Calvert Co., on Collington Branch, being part of
a tract called "Partnership." This tract was originally patented, 9 November 1680, as 1500 acres to
NICHOLAS SEWELL and JOHN DARNALL, late of Calvert
Co., deceased. The land was surveyed, 23 August
1698, and found to contain actually 1878 acres. The
land passed to said SEWELL by right of suvivorship
and he was given a patent on the land, 26 August
1699. SEWELL had previously sold 250 acres from the
lower end of this land.
Signature: NICHOLAS SEWALL
Wit.: ROBT. BRADLEY, JAMES STODDART
Ackn'd: NICHOLAS SEWELL and wife SUSANAH, 4 September 1699.
Recorded: (date unspecified), Vol. A, p. 186

Resurvey, 13 April 1698
Surveyor: THOMAS ADDISON
For: HUGH REYLEY
Property: In response to an order of the Provincial
Court dated 12 October 1697, THOMAS ADDISON resurveys
for HUGH REYLEY an 800 acre tract called "Majors
Lott" on Collington Branch. This tract bounded on
Major NICHOLAS SEWALL'S land called "Partnership."
Jurors' Signatures: THO. PINDLE, WILL. SELLBY, JOHN
BOYD, JOHN TURNER, CHA. WALLKER, JOHN CHITTAM, MAREEN
DEVALL, CHR'R THOMPSON, JOSHUA HALL, ROBT. ANDERSON,
JAMES STODDART, FFRANCIS COLLIAR.
Recorded: (date unspecified), Vol. A, p. 189

Deed, 25 January 1699
From: FFRANCIS SPRY and wife ELIZABETH of P. G. Co.
To: JOHN BIGGS of Calvert Co., planter
Price: 30 pounds sterling
Property: A 30 acre tract on the west side of Patux-
ent River, bounding on said river, Cattail Marsh, and
land of JOHN BROWNE; said land is now occupied by
said BIGGS.
Signatures: FRANCIS SPRY and ELIZABETH SPRY
Wit.: JAMES STODDERT, NICHO'S SPORNE
Ackn'd: FRANCIS SPRY and wife ELIZABETH, 25 January
1699/1700.
Recorded: (day & month unspecified) 1699/1700,
Vol. A, p. 189.

41

Deed, 4 November 1699
From: RICHARD STEPHENS of P. G. Co., planter, and
SARAH his wife.
To: SAMUELL WILLIAMS of P. G. Co.
Price: 1600 lbs. tobacco
Property: All of a 98 acre tract called "Stephens
his Hope" on the main branch of Mattawoman Creek in
P. G. Co., formerly in Charles Co., bounding on a
tract called "Smiths Choyce."
Signatures: RICH'D STEPHENS (mark), SARAH STEPHENS,
(her mark).
Wit.: WILLIAM HATTON, JOHN HAWKINS
Ackn'd: RICHARD STEPHENS, and wife SARAH, 4 November
1699.
Recorded: (no date), Vol. A, p. 191

Deed, 26 January 1698
From: JOHN WHEELER of Charles Co., planter
To: WILLIAM HUTCHISON of P. G. Co.
Price: 3000 lbs. tobacco
Property: All the 76 acre tract called "Wheelers
Adventure" in P. G. Co., formerly Charles Co., on
Pamunkey Neck by the Potomac River.
Signature: JOHN WHEELER (mark)
Wit.: WILLI. HATTON, JOHN HAWKINS
Ackn'd: JOHN WHEELER, 26 January 1698
Recorded: (no date), Vol. A, p. 192

Apprenticeship, 23 January 1699
From: BARTHOLOMEW GOFF of P. G. Co., cooper
To: CALEB NORRIS, late of Charles Co., planter
Terms: BARTHOLOMEW GOFF is to teach CALEB NORRIS
the art of cooper and carpenter and said NORRIS is
to serve him for three years, at the end of which
time, said GOFF is to provide him with a set of
carpenter's tools, "one broadaxe and saw, one carpenters adz, one froe, one drawing knife, one inch
auger, one gouge, one hammer, one chisel, one ten-
nant saw, and a good suit of cloaths." Said GOFF
is to provide food, lodging, and wearing apparel,
during NORRIS'S service.
Signatures: CALEB NORRIS, BATH. GOFF
Wit.: WILLIAM TANEYHILL, JAMES STODDART
Recorded: (no date), Vol. A, p. 193

Deed, 20 January 1699
From: JOHN HAWKINS of P. G. Co., gent., and wife
ELIZABETH.
To: RICHARD EDELIN of Charles Co.
Price: 7750 lbs. tobacco
Property: A 100 acre part of a tract called "Thomases
Chance" on Piscattaway Run in P. G. Co., being the
east half of said tract; also an adjoining 140 acre
part of a tract called "Little Ease" on the south
side of Piscattaway main fresh; said tracts having
been lately purchased from FFRANCIS MARBERY by the
said HAWKINS; the second tract bounded on "Thomases
Chance," "Locust Thickett," and Piscattaway fresh.
Signatures: JOHN HAWKINS and ELIZABETH HAWKINS
Wit.: ROBERT MIDDLETON, HICKFORD LEMON
Ackn'd: JOHN HAWKINS and wife ELIZABETH, 26 January
1699.
Recorded: (date unspecified), Vol. A, p. 194

Deed, 28 October 1699
From: THOMAS LOCKER of P. G. Co., planter
To: JOHN TALLBUTT (also spelled TALLBOT) and SARAH
his wife.
Price: "Fatherly love he beareth towards his natural
born daughter SARAH, the wife of JOHN TALLBUTT."
Property: One-half (88 acres) of a 170 acre tract
called "Langley" in P. G. Co., formerly Charles Co.,
bounding on an unnamed branch and marsh.
Signatures: THOMAS LOCKER, JOHN TALBURT
Wit.: THO. GATTON, ALEXANDER HARBERT (mark), THOMAS
NORMANSELL (his mark).
Recorded: (day & month unspecified) 1699, Vol. A,
p. 195.

Deed, 15 January 1700
From: WILLIAM CLARKSON formerly of Charles Co., now
of P. G. Co., planter.
To: ROBERT CLARKE of P. G. Co., planter
Price: 7000 lbs. tobacco
Property: All the 192 acre tract called "Clarksons
Purchase" on Broad Creek below the mouth of Clash
Creek and bounding on "Addisons Expidition" and
"Bachellors Harbour."
Signatures: WILLIAM CLARKSON, RUTH CLARKSON
Wit.: JOHN HAWKINS, ROBT. WADE
Ackn'd: WILLIAM CLARKSON and RUTH his wife, 15 Janu-
ary 1700.

Recorded: (day & month unspecified) 1699, Vol. A, p. 197.

Deed of Gift, 26 January 1699
From: CHRISTOPHER THOMPSON of P. G. Co., planter
To: "my brother" WILLIAM THOMPSON of P. G. Co., planter.
Price: Natural affection and brotherly love
Property: A 100 acre part of the 300 acre tract called "White Lackington" on the south side of the eastern branch of the Potomac River; said 100 acres being taken from the middle part of the 300 acre tract.
Signature: CHRISTOPHER THOMPSON (mark)
Wit.: JAMES BEALL, GEORGE MILLER
Ackn'd: (none)
Recorded: (day & month unspecified) 1699, Vol. A, p. 199.

Deed, 28 September 1698
From: RICHARD DURHAM, late of Calvert Co., now of London, England, carpenter; and wife.
To: JOHN TAYLOR of London, England, merchant
Price: 100 pounds sterling
Property: All the 475 acre tract called "Moores Plaines" now in P. G. Co., formerly in Calvert Co., bounding on "Thorpland" and "Brockhall." This tract was patented to JAMES MOORE in 1673 and conveyed by him to WILLIAM MELLTON, 16 June 1674. MELLTON in turn sold to said RICHARD DURHAM, 15 June 1680.
Signature: RICHARD DURHAM (mark)
Wit.: JOS. ABINGTON, GEORGE ASHMAN, BENJAMIN CHEW, and JOHN GIBSON.
Ackn'd: ALICE DURHAM wife of RICHARD DURHAM, 17 April 1699.
Recorded: (day & month unspecified) 1699, Vol. A, p. 200.

Deed, 30 November 1699
From: EDWARD FRY of Kent Co., planter
To: RICHARD JOHNS of the Cliffs in Calvert Co., merchant.
Price: 30 pounds sterling and "brotherly respect for ye avoiding of controversies & law suits that might have arisen between EDWARD FRY and RICHARD JOHNS their heirs and assigns concerning ye said two parcels of land."

Property: Two tracts called "Sway" and "Frys Choice"
totaling 800 acres on the west side of Patuxent River
adjoining land of JAMES WHITE. "Frys Choice" was a
600 acre tract in Calvert Co., originally patented to
DAVID FRY, 1 August 1673. EDWARD FRY came into the
land as next heir when DAVID FRY died intestate and
without issue. "Sway," purchased by DAVID FRY from
GEORGE YEATS of Anne Arundel Co., contained 200 acres
and bounded on Marsh Branch and Cabin Branch; it
passed to EDWARD FRY in the same manner.
Signature: EDWARD FRY
Wit.: WILL. HARRIS, EDWARD BLAY, JACOB CLULK
Ackn'd: EDWARD FRY, 30 November 1699
Recorded: (day & month unspecified) 1700, Vol. A,
p. 205.

Deed, 4 January 1699
From: THOMAS SPRIGG SENR. of P. G. Co., gent.
To: THOMAS BROOKE of P. G. Co., Esq.
Price: 50 pounds sterling
Property: A 50 acre part of the tract called "North-
ampton" in P. G. Co., bounding on "Brookes Grove."
Signature: THOMAS SPRIGG
Wit.: WILLIAM WILLKISON, CHARLES COOKE
Ackn'd: THOMAS SPRIGG SENR., 4 January 1699/1700
Recorded: (day & month unspecified) 1700, Vol. A,
p. 207.

Deed, 4 January 1699
From: THOMAS BROOKE of P. G. Co., Esq.
To: PHILLIP GETTINGS of P. G. Co., gent.
Price: 50 pounds sterling
Property: A 173 acre part of "Reparration" in P. G.
Co., bounding on "Brookes Grove" and "Repairation."
Signature: THOMAS BROOKE
Wit.: WILLIAM WILLKESON, CHARLES COOKE
Ackn'd: THOMAS BROOKE and wife BARBARA, 4 January
1699/1700.
Recorded: (day & month unspecified) 1700, Vol. A,
p. 209.

Deed, 26 March 1700
From: JOHN DEMALL of P. G. Co., planter
To: ANTHONY DRAYNE (also spelled DREINE) of P. G.
Co., planter.
Price: 32 pounds sterling and 14 shillings
Property: All the 109 acre tract called "Greenfield"

in P. G. Co., bounding on land of Capt. BROCH, JOHN
DEMALL, and WILLIAM RAYE, and on JOHN DEMALL'S Back
Branch; being part of a tract called "Something"
which was formerly surveyed for 200 acres.
Signature: JOHN DEMALL
Wit.: DAVID SMALL, EDWARD WILLETT
Ackn'd: JOHN DEMALL and wife MARY, 26 March 1700
Recorded: (day & month unspecified) 1700, Vol. A,
p. 211.

Deed, 25 March 1700
From: JOHN COUSONS of P. G. Co., planter
To: JOHN RAMSEY of P. G. Co., carpenter
Price: Love and affection
Property: A 100 acre part of "Londee" where said
COUSONS now dwells, on the north branch of Patuxent
River, being the south side of said tract.
Signature: JOHN COUSENS (mark)
Wit.: NATHANIEL WICKHAM (mark), NICHOLAS BAKER
Ackn'd: (none)
Recorded: (day & month unspecified) 1700, Vol. A,
p. 213.

Deed, 24 September 1700
From: CHRISTOPHER THOMPSON of P. G. Co., planter,
and wife GRACE.
To: JOSIAS TOWGOOD of Anne Arundel Co.
Price: 80 pounds sterling
Property: All the 200 acre tract called "Hales Rest"
in P. G. Co., formerly Calvert Co., on the west side
of Patuxent River and on the south side of Charles
Branch.
Signatures: CHRISTOP. THOMPSON (mark), GRACE THOMP-
SON (her mark).
Wit.: WILLIAM TANEYHILL, JAMES STODDART
Ackn'd: GRACE, wife of CHRISTOPHER THOMPSON, 24 Sep-
tember 1700.
Recorded: 14 October 1700, Vol. A, p. 214

Deed, 6 June 1700
From: THOMAS BROOKE of P. G. Co., Esq.
To: JOHN SMITH of P. G. Co., planter
Price: 100 pounds sterling
Property: The 12 acre and 130 acre tracts being part
of "Brookes Field" bounding on Brookes Creek Branch,
land of JOHN SMITH being also formerly part of "Brookes

Field," on land of Major NICHOLAS SEWELL, and on
Bridge Branch.
Signature: THO. BROOKE
Wit.: THO. GREENFIELD, R. BRADLY
Ackn'd: THOMAS BROOKE and wife BARBARA, 6 June 1700
Recorded: 18 October 1700, Vol. A, p. 215

Deed, 25 June 1700
From: JOHN NUTTHALL of St. Mary's Co., planter
To: THOMAS SPRIGG JR. of P. G. Co., gent.
Price: 50 pounds sterling
Property: All of a 250 acre tract at the head of
Western Branch in P. G. Co. Said tract was bequeath-
ed by THOMAS HILLARY, late of Calvert Co., deceased,
in his will dated 2 February 1697, to his wife ELINOR
who, after his death, married the said JOHN NUTWELL.
The tract was originally part of a tract called
"Three Sisters."
Signature: JOHN NUTTWELL
Wit.: MERITON, JOSIAS TOWGOOD
Ackn'd: JOHN NUTHALL and wife ELINER, 26 June 1700
Recorded: (date unspecified), Vol. A, p. 218

Deed, 24 June 1700
From: RICH'D MARSHAM of P. G. Co., gent.
To: ROBT. BRADLEY of P. G. Co., merchant
Price: 195 pounds sterling
Property: An 800 acre tract being part of "Darnalls
Grove" in P. G. Co., on the west side of Patuxent
River in the freshes and on the west side of Colling-
ton Branch where his Lordship's Manor is; and adjoin-
ing said manor.
Signature: RICHARD MARSHAM
Wit.: THOMAS HOLLYDAY, JAMES STODDERT
Ackn'd: Mrs. ANN MARSHAM, wife of RICHARD MARSHAM,
1 July (year unspecified).
Recorded: 31 October 1700, Vol. A, p. 222

99 Year Lease, 10 September 1697
From: RICHARD GROOME of P. G. Co., planter
To: CHARLES TREACY of P. G. Co., innholder
Price: 6000 lbs. tobacco and yearly rent of one ear
of Indian corn to be paid on 25th December each year.
Property: A 100 acre part of "Mt. Calvert Mannor"

in P. G. Co., at the mouth of Pig Pen Poynt Creek,
lately in the tenure of said GROOME.
Signature: RICHARD GROOME
Wit.: JOSIAS TOWGOOD, THOMAS HAWKINS
Ackn'd: RICHARD GROOME and wife (not named), 1697
Recorded: 1 November 1700, Vol. A, p. 225

95 Year Lease, 5 April 1700
From: DAVID SMALL, merchant, administrator of CHARLES
TREACY, late of P. G. Co., innholder at the time of
his decease.
To: JOSHUA CECELL of P. G. Co.
Price: 20 pounds sterling and yearly rent of one ear
of Indian corn on December 25th.
Property: A 100 acre part of "Mount CallvertMannor"
at the mouth of Pig Poynt Creek, which tract had been
leased by said TREACY from RICHARD GROOME of P. G. Co.,
planter, by deed dated 10 September 1697.
Signature: DAVID SMALL
Wit.: THOMAS CRABB, JO'N BIRD
Ackn'd: (none)
Recorded: 1 October [sic] 1700, Vol. A, p. 228

Deed, 22 June 1700
From: BENJAMIN BERRY of P. G. Co., planter
To: NINIAN BEALL of P. G. Co., gent.
Price: 40 pounds sterling
Property: All the 200 acre tract called "Berry Lott"
in the fork of the western branch of Patuxent River
in P. G. Co., formerly in Calvert Co.; being part of a
980 acre tract called "St. Andrews" laid out for
NINIAN BEALL.
Signature: BENJAMIN BERRY
Wit.: EDWARD WILLETT, ARCHIBALD EDMUNDSON
Ackn'd: BENJAMIN BERRY and wife MARY, 22 June 1700
Recorded: 2 November 1700, Vol. A, p. 230

Deed, 25 June 1700
From: NINIAN BEALL of P. G. Co., gent.
To: THOMAS PRATHER of P. G. Co.
Price: 2000 lbs. tobacco
Property: A 56 acre part of the tract called "St.
Andrews" on the north side of the western branch of
Patuxent River in the freshes, bounding on land of

WILLIAM POWELL.
Signature: NINIAN BEALL
Wit.: (none)
Ackn'd: NINIAN BEALL and wife RUTH, 25 June 1700
Recorded: 2 November 1700, Vol. A, p. 232

Deed, 25 June 1700
From: Col. NINIAN BEALL of P. G. Co., gent.
To: NATHANIEL WICKHAM of P. G. Co., planter
Price: 30 pounds sterling
Property: A 150 acre tract now called "Wickhams
Purchase" in P. G. Co. on the north side of the
western branch of Patuxent River in the freshes,
bounding on land of THOMAS BARNARD, THOMAS PRATHER,
and WILLIAM POWELL; and being part of a tract call-
ed "St. Andrews."
Signature: NINIAN BEALL
Wit.: EDWARD WILLET, ARCHIBALD EDMUNDSON
Ackn'd: NINIAN BEALL and wife RUTH, 25 June 1700
Recorded: 2 November 1700, Vol. A, p. 234

17 Year Lease, 14 September 1700
From: RICHARD GROOME of P. G. Co., planter
To: JOHN GALE of P. G. Co., planter
Price: 400 lbs. tobacco yearly for the last 13 years
of the lease, due on November 25th each year; first
payment due in 1704.
Property: A 100 acre part of "Mt. Calvert Manor" in
P. G. Co., now occupied by said GROOME; said GALE
agreed that he wants to keep no servants, not to let
any freeman farm the land during the term of the
lease; but only he himself, his wife, and children
(if he should have any), were to work the land.
Signature: RICH'D GROOME (mark)
Wit.: R. BRADLY, JOHN DODSON
Ackn'd: (none)
Recorded: (date unspecified), Vol. A, p. 236

Deed, 24 February 1699
From: JOHN CLARKE, ROBT. CLARK, BENJ. CLARKE, and
FRANCIS CLARK of Charles and St. Mary's Co.s, planters.
To: WILLIAM HERBERT of Charles Co.
Price: 8650 lbs. tobacco
Property: A 100 acre tract called "Clarkes Purchase"

in P. G. Co., on the north side of the main fresh of
Mattawoman on St. Thomases Creek, commonly known as
Notting; adjoining land of ROBT. CLARKE.
Signatures: JOHN CLARKE, ROBERT CLARKE, BENJAMIN
CLARKE, and FFRANCIS CLARKE.
Wit.: PHILLIP HOSSKINS, JAMES KEECH, BRIDGETT TAN-
DELL [BRIDGETT FENDELL].
Ackn'd: JOHN CLARK and wife ELIZABETH, ROBERT CLARK,
BENJAMIN CLARK and wife JUDITH, and FRANCIS CLARK,
24 February 1699.
Recorded: (date unspecified), Vol. A, p. 237

Deed, 29 May 1700
From: NOTTLY ROZIAR (also spelled NOTLY ROZER) of
Charles Co., gent.
To: WILLIAM CLARKSON of P. G. Co.
Price: 45 pounds sterling
Property: A 130 acre tract called "Stoney Hill" or
"Arthers Folly" being part of a tract called "Ad-
mirothona" in P. G. Co., at the head of Broad Creek,
bounding on Potomac River and on "Rozer Gifft," a
tract aliened to said CLARKSON by said ROZIAR.
Signature: NOTLEY ROZER
Wit.: WILLIAM HUTCHISON, WILLIAM CHANDLER
Ackn'd: NOTLEY ROZER, 29 May 1700
Recorded: (date unspecified), Vol. A, p. 289

Deed of Gift, 27 May 1700
From: NOTLEY ROZER of Charles Co., gent.
To: WILLIAM CLARKSON of P. G. Co. and RUTH his wife,
and after their decease, to their son WILLIAM CLARK-
SON and his heirs.
Price: Special love and favor
Property: All the 159 acre tract called "Roziars
Gift" in P. G. Co., at the main fresh that falls into
Broad Creek formerly called St. Georges Creek, being
part of a 2500 acre tract called "Admirothona."
Signature: NOTLY ROZER
Wit.: WM. HUTCHISON, WILL. CHANDLER
Ackn'd: NOTLY ROZER, 27 May 1700
Recorded: (date unspecified), Vol. A, p. 290

Deed of Exchange, 17 November 1698
From: Col. HENRY DARNALL of P. G. Co., and his wife

ELINOR.
To: CHARLES RIDGELY of Anne Arundel Co., gent.
Price: In consideration of two tracts of 500 acres
each called "Timberly" and "Generals Guift" in P. G.
Co., originally granted to ROBERT RIDGELY, late of
St. Mary's Co., deceased, and by him bequeathed to
the said CHARLES RIDGELY.
Property: All the 1100 acre tract called "Croome" on
the west side of Patuxent River and on the south side
of Charles Branch; bounding on land formerly laid out
for CHARLES BROOKE, and on St. Charles Branch; said
land lately in the tenure and occupation of one
CHARLES BUTTLER, deceased.
Signature: HENRY DARNALL
Wit.: THOMAS CLEGETT, THO. HILLS, NATHAN VEITCH
Ackn'd: "In open court," 28 August 1700
Recorded: (date unspecified), Vol. A, p. 291

Deed of Exchange, (day unspecified) November 1698
From: CHARLES RIDGELY of Anne Arundel Co., gent.,
and wife DEBORAH.
To: Col. HENRY DARNALL of P. G. Co.
Price: In exchange for the 1100 acre tract called
"Croome" in P. G. Co., originally granted to CHRISTO-
PHER ROUSBY, and lately in the tenure and occupation
of CHARLES BUTTLER, deceased.
Property: Two tracts of 500 acres each called "Timberly," and "Generals Guift," in P. G. Co., on the
west side of Patuxent River and on the south side of
St. Charles Branch; originally granted to ROBERT
RIDGELY, late of St. Mary's Co., deceased, and by
him bequeathed to the said CHARLES RIDGELY; both
tracts were formerly in Calvert Co.; "Generals Guift"
was about one mile west of land formerly laid out
for CHRISTOPHER ROUSBY called "Croome"; "Timberly"
bounded on "Generals Guift" and on said ROUSBY'S
land.
Signature: CHARLES RIDGELY
Wit.: THOMAS CLEGGETT, NATHAN VEITCH, THOMAS HILLS
Ackn'd: "In open court," 28 August 1700
Recorded: (date unspecified), Vol. A, p. 293

Deed, 24 February 1699
From: JOHN CLARK, ROBT. CLARKE, BENJAMIN CLARK, and
FFRANCIS CLARK of Charles and St. Mary's Co., planters.

To: JOHN COURTS (also spelled COATS, COARTS), of
Charles Co., gent.
Price: 8250 lbs. tobacco
Property: All the tract called "Crouches Guift" in
P. G. Co., on the north side of the main fresh on
the head of Mattawoman or St. Thomases Creek common-
ly known by the name of Notting, bounding on land of
JOHN CLARKE; 500 acres.
Signatures: JOHN CLARKE, ROBT. CLARKE, BENJ'N CLARK,
FFRANCIS CLARK.
Wit.: PHILL. HOSKINS, JAMES KEECH, and BRIDGETT FFEN-
DALL (her mark).
Ackn'd: JOHN CLARKE and wife ELIZABETH, ROBERT CLARKE,
BENJAMIN CLARKE and wife JUDITH, and FFRANCIS CLARKE,
27 February 1699.
Recorded: 14 November 1700, Vol. A, p. 293-A

Deed, 8 January 1699
From: WILLIAM HUTCHESON and wife SARAH, and ROB'T
MIDDLETON and wife MARY, both of P. G. Co.
To: FFRANCIS MARBURY of P. G. Co.
Price: 20,000 lbs. tobacco
Property: All the tract called "Apple Hill" in P. G.
Co., bounding on "Exeter" laid out for JOHN WHEELER
on the north side of Piscattaway main branch; 522
acres.
Signatures: WILLIAM HUTCHISON, SARAH HUTCHISON,
ROBERT MIDDLTON, MARY MIDDLETON.
Wit.: RICH'D EDELIN, HICKFORD LEMAN
Ackn'd: WILLIAM HUTCHISON and wife SARAH; ROBERT
MIDDLETON and wife MARY; 20 January 1699.
Recorded: (date unspecified), Vol. A, p. 295

Deed, 18 September 1700
From: RICHARD ISAAK of P. G. Co., "tayler"
To: JOSHUA HALL of P. G. Co., planter
Price: 18,000 lbs. tobacco
Property: All the tract "Giants Range" in P. G. Co.,
on the west side of Patuxent River in the freshes and
on the eastern most fork of said river bounding on
land of JAMES WILLIAMS called "Penthen Hills" and on
"Collington"; 100 acres.
Signature: RICHARD ISAAK
Wit.: JOSEPH BROWNE (mark), BENJ. BERRY
Ackn'd: RICHARD ISAAK, 24 September 1700

Recorded: (date unspecified), Vol. A, p. 296

Deed, 28 November 1699
From: THOMAS STOCKET of Anne Arundel Co., gent., as
Executor of the last will and testament of MARY YATE,
late of Anne Arundel Co., widow.
To: THOMAS JAMES of P. G. Co., planter
Price: 1200 lbs. tobacco
Property: Part of "The Vale of Benjamin" in P. G.
Co., bounding on land of CHARLES WILLIAM'S, and on
Turkey Branch; 30 acres.
Signature: THOMAS STOCKET
Wit.: ROBT. TYLER, JAMES STODDERT
Ackn'd: THOMAS STOCKETT, 28 November 1699
Recorded: (date unspecified), Vol. A, p. 298

Deed, 8 April 1699
From: GEORGE LINGAN of Calvert Co., gent., and wife
ANN.
To: JOSIAH WILLSON of Calvert Co., gent., and MARTHA
his wife, one of the daughters of the said LINGAN.
Price: Love and affection
Property: The southern half of the 380 acre tract
called "Buttington," originally in Calvert Co., on
the west side of Patuxent River in the branches of
Ffordsham Creek, bounding on land of JOHN BOYNE
called "Redding"; originally granted to LINGAN on
15 March 1665.
Signatures: GEORGE LINGAN, ANN LINGAN
Wit.: JOHN TASKER, SAM'LL PETER
Ackn'd: GEORGE LINGAN and wife ANN, 8 April 1699
Recorded: (date unspecified), Vol. A, p. 299

Deed, 27 August 1700
From: Col. NINIAN BEALL of P. G. Co., gent.
To: ELIZABETH BELT of Anne Arundel Co.
Price: 120 pounds sterling
Property: Part of "Good Luck" in P. G. Co. in the
freshes of the western branch of Patuxent River on
the north side of Beaver Dam Branch, bounding on
THOMAS HILLARY'S land called "Three Sisters," 100
acres; also all the tract called "The Addition to
Good Luck," bounding on "Good Luck"; 200 acres.
Signature: NINIAN BEALL

Wit.: (none)
Ackn'd: Col. NINIAN BEALL and wife RUTH, 27 August
1700.
Recorded: 10 February 1700, Vol. A, p. 302

Deed, 25 November 1700
From: NICHOLAS BRENT of Colony of Virginia, gent.,
Executor of the last will and testament of GEORGE
BRENT, late of Virginia, deceased.
To: Hon. Col. HENRY DARNALL of P. G. Co.
Price: 80 pounds sterling
Property: All the tract "Pitchcraft" in P. G. Co.,
formerly in Calvert Co., on the west side of Patuxent
River on the south side of land laid out for CHRISTO-
PHER ROUSBY, gent., called "Croome," bounding on land
of CHARLES BROOKE, JOHN BIGGER'S "Too Good," and ROB-
ERT RIDGLY'S "Timberly"; 400 acres.
Signature: NICHOLAS BRENT
Wit.: CHARLES CARROLL, CLEMENT HILL JUN'R, JOHN FFEN-
WICK.
Ackn'd: (none)
Recorded: 10 February 1700, Vol. A, p. 305

Deed, 19 February 1699
From: FFRANCIS MARBURY of P. G. Co., planter, and
his wife MARY.
To: JOHN HAWKINS of P. G. Co.
Price: 10,000 lbs. tobacco
Property: One-half of "Thomasses Chance" in P. G.
Co., lately purchased from EDWARD SCOTT by the said
MARBURY and MORRIS LOYD, lately deceased, by inden-
ture dated 20 November 1700; tract bounds on Piscatt-
away Run, 100 acres; also the tract "Little Ease,"
lately purchased by said MARBURY from WM. HARBERT of
Charles Co., by indenture dated 20 November (year un-
specified); said tract is in P. G. Co. and bounds on
"Thomasses Chance," and "Locust Thicket"; 200 acres.
Signatures: FFRANCIS MARBURY, MARY MARBURY
Wit.: HICKFORD LEMON, RICH'D EDELIN
Ackn'd: FFRANCIS MARBURY and wife MARY, 20 January
1699.
Recorded: 11 February 1700, Vol. A, p. 307

Deed, 22 June 1700

From: Col. NINIAN BEALL of P. G. Co., gent.
To: BENJAMIN HADDOCK of England, mariner
Price: 11,250 lbs. tobacco
Property: A 456 acre part of the tract called "In-
closure" in P. G. Co. on the north side of the east-
ern branch of the Potomac River, bounding on Lyle's
Branch.
Signature: NINIAN BEALL
Wit.:   EDWARD WILLETT, ARCHIBALD EDMUNDSON
Ackn'd: NINIAN BEALL and wife RUTH, 22 June 1700
Recorded: 11 February 1700, Vol. A, p. 309

Deed, 26 August 1700
From: GEORGE SPICER of Calvert Co., planter
To: CHARLES STRAWBERRY of Calvert Co., "his Godson"
Price: Respect and consideration
Property: A 100 acre part of the tract called "Col-
lins Comfort" in P. G. Co. on the west side of the
Patuxent River in the freshes between Deep Creek and
Mattapony Creek; being part of a 250 acre parcel
originally laid out to GEORGE COLLINS, late of said
county, deceased; said property was conveyed to said
SPICER by deed of WM. COLLINS, grandson of said
GEORGE COLLINS; said STRAWBERRY is not to have use
of the property until the expiration of an indenture
of sale made between said GEORGE SPICER and THOMAS
BRATT, alias BRIDGES, of P. G. Co.
Signature: GEORGE SPICER
Wit.:   ED. BATTSON, JOHN GOSLING
Ackn'd: GEORGE SPICER, 27 August 1700
Recorded: 11 February 1700, Vol. A, p. 311

Deed, 1 July 1700
From: JOHN SMITH of P. G. Co., planter
To: WILLIAM BARTON of P. G. Co., gent.
Price: 60 pounds sterling
Property: One-half (250 acres) of a 500 acre tract
called "The Exchange" in P. G. Co. at the head of
Deep Creek bounding on Mattapony Old Indian Path and
land of Mr. RICHARD MARSHAM. Said tract was original-
ly granted to JOHN BOWLING and JOHN KING; JOHN SMITH
conveyed the tract to MURPHY WARD, 1 September 1684;
WARD had the tract resurveyed and sold it to the
said JOHN SMITH, 15 March 1686.
Signature: JOHN SMITH
Wit.:   NICH'S SPORNE, JOHN SIMPSON

Ackn'd: JOHN SMITH and wife ANN, 1 July 1700
Recorded: (date unspecified), Vol. A, p. 314

Deed, 24 May 1700
From: JOHN BOWLING of Calvert Co., planter
To: WM. BARTON of P. G. Co., gent.
Price: 40 pounds sterling
Property: All the tract (500 acres) called "The Ex-
change" in P. G. Co. on the south side of Deep Creek
and on the west side of Patuxent River; being a tract
originally granted to JOHN BOWLING and JOHN KING on
26 May 1664. KING died without issue and the tract
passed to said BOWLING. After BOWLING'S decease, the
tract passed to his heir, the said JOHN BOWLING.
Signature: JOHN BOWLING (mark)
Wit.: WILLIAM CLARKE, JOSH. CECILL
Ackn'd: JOHN BOWLING and wife MARY, 24 May 1700
Recorded: 11 February 1700, Vol. A, p. 317

Deed, 10 June 1700
From: Col. HENRY JOWLES of St. Mary's Co.
To: JOSHUA CECELL of P. G. Co.
Price: 50 pounds sterling
Property: All the 500 acre tract called "Grove Hurst,"
formerly in Charles Co., now in P. G. Co., at the
head of Beaver Dam Branch on the eastern branch of
Potomac River, adjoining land of HENRY LOW. Said
land was originally patented to Col. HENRY JOWLES on
10 December 1686.
Signature: HEN. JOWLES
Wit.: HENRY BONNER, E. BATSON
Ackn'd: Col. HENRY JOWLES and wife SIBLE, 10 June 1700
Recorded: 13 February 1700, Vol. A, p. 320

Quit Claim Deed, 20 April 1700
From: JACOB MOORLAND (also spelled MOORELAND), of
St. Mary's Co.
To: JOSHUA CECELL of P. G. Co.
Price: "A competent sum"
Property: All right and title to the 500 acre tract
called "Grove Hurst."
Signature: JACOB MORLAND
Wit.: HENRY JOWLES, HENRY JOWLES, JR.
Ackn'd: (none)
Recorded: 17 February 1700, Vol. A, p. 323

Quit Claim Deed, 14 July 1700
From: DAVID SMALL of P. G. Co., merchant
To: Capt. THOMAS EMMS of London, England; mariner
Price: 150 pounds sterling
Property: Two parcels taken from "Calvert Mannor" on
Calvert Branch on the west side of Patuxent River in
the freshes near the dividing thereof. 1) A 163 acre
tract, except for lots already built upon according
to an act of the Assembly creating a town [Charles
Town] from "Mount Calvert Manor," and also one acre
leased by WILLIAM and MARY GROOME to JOSIAS TOWGOOD
for 99 years. Said tract bounding on land of JOHN
DAVIS, CHRISTOPHER BAINES, and CHARLES TRACEY, the
main road to the ferry, and the great sunken marsh.
2) A 250 acre tract bounding on land of Mr. BRADLEY,
RICHARD GROOME, and CHARLES TRACEY. "Mount Calvert
Mannor," containing 1000 acres, was granted to PHIL-
LIP CALVERT of St. Mary's Co., 17 February 1658.
CALVERT conveyed the land to WILLIAM GROOME of Calvert Co. from whom it passed by bequest to GROOME'S
eldest son WILLIAM GROOME who was to give half of
the tract to his brother RICHARD GROOME. WILLIAM
GROOME of Charlestown, P. G. Co., innholder, and
his wife MARY, conveyed their interest in the prop-
erty, 24 July 1690, to THOMAS EMMS, of London,
mariner, and DAVID SMALL of P. G. Co., merchant.
Signature: DAVID SMALL
Wit.: JOHN BATTE, EDW'D BATTSON
Ackn'd: DAVID SMALL, 14 July 1700
Recorded: 18 February 1700, Vol. A, p. 324

94 Year Lease, 14 July 1700
From: DAVID SMALL of P. G. Co., merchant, Administrator of CHARLES TRACEY, late of Charlestown, innholder, deceased.
To: Capt. THOMAS EMMS of London, England; mariner
Price: 50 pounds sterling and yearly rent of one
grain of wheat paid December 25th.
Property: A tract of 2 acres and 72 perches taken
from "Mount Calvert Mannor" on the west side of
Patuxent River in the freshes near the dividing of
the river. Said "Mount Calvert Mannor" was granted
to PHILLIP CALVERT, 17 February 1658, and from CAL-
VERT, the land passed to WILLIAM GROOME and MARY his
wife (see Deed, SMALL to EMMS, 14 July 1700), who
conveyed said 2 acres and 72 perches to CHARLES
TRACEY by 99 Year Lease dated 28 September 1695.

CHARLES TRACEY died leaving neither wife nor issue and the property passed to DAVID SMALL, his greatest creditor.
Signature: DAVID SMALL
Wit.: JOHN BATIE, EDW'D BATTSON
Ackn'd: DAVID SMALL, 17 July 1700
Recorded: 19 February 1700, Vol. A, p. 329

Deed, 29 November 1699
From: ROBERT LILE (also spelled LYLE) of Calvert Co., planter.
To: ELIZABETH MORLEY, Executrix of the last will and testament of GRIFFIN MORLEY of Anne Arundel Co., deceased.
Price: 45 pounds sterling
Property: A 200 acre part of a tract called "Waughton" on the eastern branch of the Potomac River. In 1687, a 492 acre tract called "Waughtown" in Charles Co., bounding on a tract called "Cuckhold Delight," and on land of BENJAMIN HADDOCK, was granted to WILLIAM LYLE, late of Calvert Co., deceased, ("see survey of 4 August 1686"). WILLIAM LYLE died intestate and the tract passed to his eldest son ROBERT LYLE of Calvert Co. who contracted to sell 200 acres of the land to the said GRIFFIN MORLEY, 18 May 1698. Said land was bequeathed by said MORLEY in his will dated 9 August 1699.
Signature: ROBERT LYLE
Wit.: JOHN BATTIE, ANDREW HAMBLETON
Ackn'd: ROBERT LYLE and wife ELIZABETH, 29 November 1699.
Recorded: 19 February 1700, Vol. A, p. 332

Deed, 29 November 1699
From: ROBERT LYLE of Calvert Co., planter
To: JOHN HUGGINS of Anne Arundel Co., planter
Price: 35 pounds sterling
Property: A 292 acre part of the tract called "Waughtown" on the east branch of the Potomac River bounding on "Cuckholds Delight" and on the said land of BENJAMIN HADDOCK [see above deed: LYLE to MORLEY, 29 November 1699].
Signatures: ROBERT LYLE, ELIZABETH LYLE
Wit.: JOHN BATTIE, ANDREW HAMBLETON
Ackn'd: ROBERT LYLE and wife ELIZABETH, (no date)

Recorded: 21 February 1700, Vol. A, p. 335

Deed, 24 September 1700
From: EDWARD BATTSON of Calvert Co., gent.
To: SAMUEL HOLDSWORTH of Calvert Co., gent.
Price: 4000 lbs. tobacco
Property: All the 70 acre tract called "Yarmouth"
in P. G. Co. on the south side of the Patuxent River
on the western branch, bounding on a tract called
"Bacon Hill," now in the possession of Maj. NINIAN
BEALL and on "Mussellshell" late in the possession
of FFRANCIS SWINSEN.
Signature: E. BATTSON
Wit.: WILLIAM BARTON, BENJ'A BERRY
Ackn'd: "In open court," 24 September [1700]
Recorded: (date not specified), Vol. A, p. 337

Deed, 24 June 1700
From: RICHARD MARSHAM of P. G. Co., gent.
To: ROBERT TYLER of P. G. Co., gent.
Price: 650 pounds sterling
Property: The 3000 acre tract called "Darnalls
Grove" in P. G. Co. on the west side of the Patuxent
River in the freshes on the west side of Collington
Branch where his Lordship's mannor is; being part of
what was originally a 3800 acre tract.
Signature: RICHARD MARSHAM
Wit.: THOMAS HOLLYDAY, JAMES STODDORT
Ackn'd: ANN MARSHAM, wife of RICHARD, 1 July 1700
Recorded: 21 February 1700, Vol. A, p. 338

Deed, 28 January 1700
From: JAMES STODDART of P. G. Co., gent.
To: JOSEPH CHEW of Anne Arundel Co., gent.
Price: 123 pounds sterling
Property: All the 500 acre tract called "Yarrow" in
P. G. Co. on the north side of the eastern branch of
Potomac River, bounding on land of WILLIAM THOMPSEN;
also a 506 acre tract called "Yarrow Head" on the
north side of the eastern branch of the Potomac River,
bounding on land of GEORGE MILLER, and intersecting
said STODDART'S land where he now lives.
Signature: JAMES STODDART
Wit.: THOMAS HOLLYDAY, RO'T BRADLY

Ackn'd: JAMES STODDART and wife MARY, 25 January
1700.
Recorded: (date unspecified), Vol. A, p. 340

Deed, 27 November 1700
From: JOHN SMITH of P. G. Co., planter
To: JAMES STODDART of P. G. Co., gent.
Price: 100 pounds sterling
Property: A 50 acre part of a tract called "Long
Looked For" in P. G. Co. on the south main branch
of Deep Creek bounding on land formerly laid out for
Maj. THOMAS BROOK called "Little Grove," and on land
of RICHARD MARSHAM; also a 200 acre part of which
was formerly granted to Maj. THOMAS BROOK and is now
in possession of MURPHEY WARD, and part of which was
granted to MURPHY WARDE, called "Wards Pasture"; the
second tract is on the west side of the Patuxent River
in P. G. Co. on Deep Creek, and bounds on "Little
Grove" and on land of GEORGE LINGAN being part of
"Long Looked For."
Signature: JOHN SMITH
Wit.:   WILLIAM TANYHILL, R. BRADLEY
Ackn'd: ANN SMITH, wife of JOHN, 27 November 1700
Recorded: 24 February 1700, Vol. A, p. 343

Deed, 13 January 1700
From: RICHARD ISACK of P. G. Co., "taylor"
To: EDWARD HOLMES of P. G. Co., planter
Price: 150 pounds sterling
Property: All the 135 acre tract called "Plummers
Pleasure" in P. G. Co. between the north branch of
Patuxent River and Collington Branch; bounding on
"Lundy," "Cuckholds Delight," and "Mount Pleasant";
also all the 46 acre tract called "Addition to
"Plummers Pleasure."
Signature: RICH'D ISAAC
Wit.:   MATTHEW MACKBEE (mark), JOSEPH BROWNE (mark)
Ackn'd: RICHARD ISAAC, 13 January 1700
Recorded: 25 February 1700, Vol. A, p. 345

Bond, 13 January 1700
From: RICHARD ISACK of P. G. Co., "taylor"
To: EDWARD HOLMES of P. G. Co., planter
Price: 300 pounds sterling

Terms: Said ISACK bound to observe the conditions
of a deed bearing the same date conveying land to said
HOLMES or pay HOLMES the 300 pounds sterling.
Signature: RICHARD ISACK
Wit.: ROB'T TYLER, THO. SPRIG, JR.
Recorded: 25 February 1700, Vol. A, p. 347

Deed, 27 January 1700
From: THOMAS GREENFEILD of P. G. Co., planter
To: GEORGE JONES of P. G. Co., planter
Price: 8000 lbs. tobacco
Property: The upper half (100 acres) of the 200
acre tract called "Quick Sale" on the north side
of Patuxent River at the head of a tract of land
formerly granted to ROBERT TAYLOR; said tract having
been "aliented" by FFRANCIS STREET to WILLIAM COLLINS,
deceased, as shown in Calvert Co. records; also the
eastern part of a tract called "Gedling" bounding on
COLLIN'S land, "Quick Sale," and on ALEXANDER MAGRUD-
ER'S land called "Anchovis Hill."
Signature: THOMAS GREENFEILD
Wit.: T. TRUMAN GREENFEILD, JAMES GREENFEILD
Ackn'd: MARTHA, wife of THOMAS GREENFEILD, 27 January 1700.
Recorded: 25 February 1700, Vol. A, p. 348

Deed, 3 January 1700
From: ROBERT TYLER of P. G. Co., gent.
To: RICHARD BUTT of Anne Arundel Co., planter
Price: 69 pounds sterling
Property: All the 206 and 1/4 acre tract called
"Batchelors Delight" recently purchased by said TYLER
from RICHARD MARSHAM, said tract being part of the
3800 acre tract called "Darnalls Grove," formerly
in Calvert Co., now in P. G. Co., on the west side
of Collington Branch; bounding on "Darnalls Grove,"
and land of SAMUEL DUVALL and ROBERT BRADLY.
Signature: ROB'T TYLER
Wit.: RICHARD DUCKETT, LEWIS DUVALL
Ackn'd: ROBERT TYLER and wife SUSANNA, 3 January
1700.
Recorded: 25 February 1700, Vol. A, p. 349

Deed, 29 January 1700

61

From: WILLIAM THOMPSON of P. G. Co., planter; and
wife ANN.
To: GEORGE MILLER of P. G. Co.
Price: 6000 lbs. tobacco
Property: All the 300 acre tract called "Scottland"
in P. G. Co., formerly in Charles Co., on the west
side of Eastern Branch; bounding on the river and
land of RICHARD EVANS.
Signature: WILLIAM THOMPSON
Wit.: WILLIAM HUTCHISON, WILL. TANYHILL
Ackn'd: WILLIAM THOMPSON, 29 January 1700
Recorded: 25 February 1700, Vol. A, p. 352

Deed, 26 March 1701
From: JOHN NUTTWELL of St. Mary's Co., planter;
and wife ELINOR.
To: THOMAS SPRIGG, JR. of P. G. Co., gent.
Price: 50 pounds sterling
Property: A 250 acre part of the tract called
"Three Sisters" in P. G. Co. at the head of Western
Branch; said tract having been bequeathed by THOMAS
HILLARY, late of Calvert Co., deceased, by will dated
2 February 1697, to said ELINOR who was then his wife.
Signatures: JOHN NUTTWELL, JR., ELINOR NUTTWELL
(her mark).
Wit.: ROB'T BRADLEY, ROB'T WADE
Ackn'd: JO'N NUTTWELL, and wife ELINOR, 26 March
1701.
Recorded: 3 May 1701, Vol. A, p. 354

Deed, 26 March 1701
From: THOMAS SPRIGG, JR. of P. G. Co., gent.
To: Maj. WALLTER SMITH of Calvert Co., gent.
Price: 61 pounds sterling
Property: A 250 part of "Three Sisters" in P. G. Co.
at the head of Western Branch; said land was former-
ly bequeathed by THOMAS HILLERY in his will dated
2 February 1697, to ELINOR his wife who, after his
decease, married JOHN NUTTWELL; said tract was con-
veyed to said THOMAS SPRIGG, JR. by JOHN NUTTWELL
and wife ELINOR, 26 March 1701.
Signature: THOMAS SPRIG
Wit.: ROB'T BRADLY, ROB'R WADE
Ackn'd: THOMAS SPRIGG, JR. and wife MARGRETT, 26
March 1701.

Recorded: (no date specified), Vol. A, p. 357

Deed, 25 March 1701
From: ROBERT BRADLY of P. G. Co., gent.
To: THOMAS ODELL of Anne Arundel Co., gent.
Price: 350 pounds sterling
Property: An 800 acre part of the tract called
"Darnalls Grove" in P. G. Co. on the west side of
Patuxent River in the freshes, on the west side of
Collington Branch.
Signature: ROB'T BRADLEY
Wit.: THOMAS SPRIGG, JAMES STODDART
Ackn'd: (none)
Recorded: (no date specified), Vol. A, p. 359

Deed of Gift, 16 March 1700
From: THOMAS SPRIGG, SR. of P. G. Co., gent.
To: SARAH PEARCE, eldest daughter of THOMAS SPRIGG,
SR.; and JOHN PEARCE, grandson of THOMAS SPRIGG, SR.,
and son of said SARAH, of P. G. Co., planters
Price: Love and affection
Property: A 200 acre part of the 1000 acre tract
called "Northampton" and the 325 acre tract called
"Kettering" on the west side of the Western Branch
of Patuxent River; said 200 acres lately being in
the tenure of JOHN SPRIGG, deceased. "Northampton"
was originally granted to THOMAS SPRIGG, SR., 1 March
1673 and "Kettering" was originally granted to him,
1 August 1686. SARAH PEARCE to have use of the land
during her natural life, then to her son JOHN PEARCE
and his wife, then to the heirs of said JOHN PEARCE,
if none, then to SARAH BELL, wife of JAMES BELL and
daughter of said SARAH PEARCE, then to heirs of SARAH
BELL, if none, then to heirs of THOMAS SPRIGG.
Signature: THOMAS SPRIGG
Wit.: EDWARD WILLETT, SUSANNA JOYCE (mark)
Ackn'd: THOMAS SPRIGG, SR., 16 March 1700
Recorded: (no date specified), Vol. A, p. 361

Deed, 24 February 1700
From: THOMAS BROOKE of P. G. Co., Esq.
To: CLEMENT HILL of P. G. Co., gent.
Price: 50 pounds sterling and 3000 lbs. tobacco
Property: A 200 acre part of the 547 acre tract

called "The Forest" in P. G. Co. on Piscattaway
Branch, bounding on land surveyed for Col. HENRY
DARNALL, and said DARNALL'S tract "Exchange." Said
tract was originally granted to said THOMAS BROOKE.
Signature: THO'S BROOKE
Wit.: NT. SMITH, WM. BARTON
Ackn'd: THOMAS BROOKE and wife BARBARA, 20 February
1700.
Recorded: 20 June 1701, Vol. A, p. 364

Deed, 26 June 1700
From: JAMES MOORE of P. G. Co., carpenter
To: ROBERT ORME of P. G. Co., planter
Price: 10,000 lbs. tobacco paid to HUGH JONES of
P. G. Co., planter, by JAMES MOOR.
Property: All the 125 acre tract called "Dunbarr"
in P. G. Co., formerly in Calvert Co., on the west
side of Patuxent River bounding on Mattapony Branch,
land of GEORGE YOUNG, and on "Essex Lodge."
Signature: JAMES MOORE
Wit.: ROBERT BRADLY, JAMES STODDART, JOSH. CECELL
Ackn'd: JAMES MOORE and wife MARY, 26 June 1700
Recorded: 20 June 1701, Vol. A, p. 365

Deed, 12 April 1701
From: ELIZABETH BELLT of Anne Arundel Co., widow
To: JOSEPH BELT of P. G. Co., second son of said
ELIZABETH BELLT.
Price: Natural affection and a competent "maintain-
ances," and considering that said JOSEPH BELT is
grown to the age and maturity of managing the affairs
of the country, and in consideration of the fact
that said JOSEPH BELT has released his title to a
tract called "Friends Choyce" to said ELIZABETH
BELT by deed dated 12 April 1701.
Property: A 150 acre parcel consisting of parts of
the tracts "Good Luck," and the addition to this tract
called "Widows Purchase," lying in P. G. Co. on the
forks of the west branch of Patuxent River and on
the north side of Beaver Damm Branch, bounding on
THOMAS HILLARY'S tract "Three Sisters," and "Addition
to Good Luck." The part of "Good Luck" conveyed to
said JOSEPH BELT had been willed to him by his father
JOHN BELT, to be received after the decease of his
mother, the said ELIZABETH BELT.

Signature: ELIZABETH BELT
Wit.: ROBERT TYLER, THOMAS SPRIGG, JUNR.
Ackn'd: ELIZABETH BELT, 12 April 1701
Recorded: 21 June 1701, Vol. A, p. 368

Deed, 22 May 1696
From: WILLIAM HERBERT of Charles Co., planter
To: DANIEL JENKINSON of Charles Co., planter
Price: 9000 lbs. tobacco
Property: All the 285 acre tract called "Gods Guift"
in P. G. Co., formerly in Charles Co., on Piscatta-
way Creek on the north side of the main fresh run-
ning into Piscattaway Creek, bounding on an Indian
field. Said land was originally granted to RICHARD
FAULKS of Charles Co., deceased.
Signatures: WILLIAM HARBERT, MARY HERBERT (mark)
Wit.: JOSIAS TOWGOOD, WILLIAM CLARKSON
Ackn'd: WILLIAM HERBERT and wife MARY, 22 May 1699
Recorded: 21 June 1701, Vol. A, p. 372

Deed, 15 February 1700
From: JAMES MOOR of P. G. Co., gent.
To: EDWARD WILLETT of P. G. Co., pewterer
Price: 5200 lbs. tobacco
Property: A 157 acre part of the 300 acre tract
called "The Horse Race" bounding on "Bealls Craft"
which is already in possession of EDWARD WILLETT,
on land of Col. JOHN BIGGAR'S, and on Western Branch.
Signature: JAMES MOORE
Wit.: (none)
Ackn'd: JAMES MOORE and wife MARY, 15 February 1700
Recorded: 21 June 1701, Vol. A, p. 374

Deed, 15 February 1700
From: JAMES MOOR of P. G. Co., gent.
To: THOMAS BOX of P. G. Co., blacksmith
Price: 5500 lbs. tobacco
Property: A 163 acre part of the 300 acre tract
called "The Horse Race" lying on Cabbin Branch,
bounding on Col. JOHN BIGGAR'S land in Cabbin Branch,
on EDWARD WILLETT'S part of "The Horse Race," and on
Western Branch.
Signature: JAMES MOORE
Wit.: THOMAS HOLLYDAY, ROBT. BRADLY

Ackn'd: JAMES MOOR and wife MARY, 15 February 1700
Recorded: 21 June 1701, Vol. A, p. 376

Deed, 21 June 1701
From: ALLEXANDER MAGRUDER and NATHANIELL MAGRUDER,
both of P. G. Co., gent.
To: SAM'LL MAGRUDER of P. G. Co.
Price: 34 pounds sterling
Property: A 100 acre part of "Charighigth" now call-
ed "Magruders Delight," bounding on SAMUEL MAGRUD-
ER'S land "Good Luck."
Signatures: ALLEXANDER MAGRUDER, NATHANIELL MAGRUDER
Wit.: JO. HAWKINS, HICKFORD LEMAN
Ackn'd: ALLEXANDER MAGRUDER and wife ANN, and NA-
THANIELL MAGRUDER, 24 June 1701.
Recorded: 4 July 1701, Vol. A, p. 379

Deed, 25 June 1701
From: NINIAN BEALL of P. G. Co., gent.
To: SAMUEL MAGRUDER of P. G. Co., planter
Price: 81 pounds sterling and 4 shillings
Property: All the 325 acre tract "Troublesome" on
the north side of the southwest branch of the western
branch of Patuxent River, bounding on land of Mr.
• CHARLES CARROLL, and on "Bealls Guift."
Signature: NINIAN BEALL
Wit.: THOM. HOLLYDAY, EDWARD WILLETT
Ackn'd: NINIAN BEALL and wife RUTH, 25 June 1701
Recorded: (date unspecified), Vol. A, p. 381

Deed, 15 April 1701
From: NATHANIELL MAGRUDER of P. G. Co.
To: THOMAS GREENFEILD of P. G. Co.
Price: Valuable consideration
Property: A 28 acre piece from the southwestern
part of "Anchovis Hills" bounding on said GREENFEILD'S
tract called "Compass Hills," on "Popplar Hill," and
on Aquasto Branch.
Signature: NATHANIELL MAGRUDER (mark)
Wit.: THOMAS STOTT, HERMANN LEFEVER
Ackn'd: NATHANIEL MAGRUDER, 24 June 1701
Recorded: (date unspecified), Vol. A, p. 383

Deed, 16 April 1701
From: WILLIAM MILLS of P. G. Co., planter
To: WILLIAM WATTSON of P. G. Co., planter
Price: 6274 lbs. tobacco
Property: An 87 acre piece of the southwestern
part of "Trenant."
Signature: WILLIAM MILLS (mark)
Wit.: THOMAS GREENFEILD, JOHN WIGHT
Ackn'd: WILLIAM MILLS and wife ELIZABETH, 16 April
1701.
Recorded: 9 July 1701, Vol. A, p. 384

Deed, 31 August 1700
From: PHILLIP LYNES of Charles Co., gent., and wife
MARGARETT.
To: HICKFORD LEMAN of P. G. Co.
Price: 127 pounds sterling
Property: The southern half of the 800 acre tract
"Batchelors Harbour" in P. G. Co., formerly in Charles
Co., on the east side of Piscattaway River about two
miles above Piscattaway Creek, bounding on St. George
Creek, Ash Creek, and Jeroms Creek which is also
called Swan Creek.
Signature: PHILIP LYNES
Wit.: JOHN HAWKINS, ROBT. WADE, JOHN BALDWIN
Ackn'd: PHILLIP LYNES, 31 August 1700
Recorded: (date unspecified), Vol. A, p. 385

Deed, 1 May 1701
From: JOHN ADDISON of P. G. Co., and wife REBECCA;
and WILLIAM HUTCHISON of P. G. Co., and wife SARAH.
To: JAMES GREEN of P. G. Co., and THOMAS FREDERICK
of P. G. Co.
Price: 15,000 lbs. tobacco
Property: All the 600 acre tract "Strife" in P. G.
Co. on the north side of Mattawoman Branch, bounding
on the main road from Piscattaway to Port Tobacco
now called the lower road, and on the upper road to
Port Tobacco.
Signatures: JNO. ADDISON, WM. HUTCHISON
Wit.: WILLIAM TANYHILL, ROBT. WADE
Ackn'd: JOHN ADDISON, Esq., and wife REBECCA; and
WILLIAM HUTCHISON and wife SARAH, 1 May 1701.
Recorded: 9 July 1701, Vol. A, p. 387

Deed, 24 June 1601 [sic]
From: Mr. EDWARD BALL of Calvert Co., gent.
To: SAMUEL LYLE of P. G. Co.
Price: 50 pounds sterling
Property: All the 200 acre tract "Cuckholds Delight"
in P. G. Co. on the north side of the eastern branch
of the Potomac River, bounding on land of JAMES MULLI-
KIN, being land originally patented to THOMAS GREEN.
Signature: EDWARD BALL (mark)
Wit.: EDWARD WILLETT, BENJAMIN BRASHEER
Ackn'd: EDWARD BALL and wife PRISSILLA, 24 June 1701
Recorded: 9 July 1701, Vol. A, p. 388

Deed, 31 July 1699
From: JOHN TAYLOR of London, England, merchant, and
wife MARGARET.
To: NATHAN SMITH of Maryland, merchant
Price: 100 pounds sterling
Property: All the 475 acre tract "Moores Plaines"
in Calvert Co., bounding on "Thorpland" and "Brooke-
hall," being land originally patented to JAMES MOORE,
1 August 1673, who conveyed the land by deed dated
16 June 1674 to WILLIAM MELLTON who conveyed it by
deed dated 16 June 1680 to RICHARD DURHAM who conveyed
the land by deed, 28 September 1698, to said JOHN
TAYLOR.
Signatures: JOHN TAILLOR, MARGRETT TAILLOR
Wit.: (none)
Ackn'd: JOHN TAYLOR and wife MARGRETT, 31 July 1699
Recorded: 11 July 1701, Vol. A, p. 390

Deed, 26 April 1700
From: ROBERT TYLER of P. G. Co., gent.
To: RICHARD ROBSON of P. G. Co., planter
Price: 7000 lbs. tobacco
Property: A 103 acre part of "Darnalls Groave" in
P. G. Co. bounding on land of SAMUEL FARMER and
ROBERT BRADLEY.
Signature: ROBERT TYLER
Wit.: THOMAS SPRIGG, RICH'D CLARKE
Ackn'd: Mr. ROBERT TYLER and wife SUSANNA, 26 April
1701.
Recorded: 11 July 1701, Vol. A, p. 393

Deed, 28 February 1699
From: EDWARD BOTELER of Calvert Co., gent.

To: WILLIAM LOW of P. G. Co., planter
Price: 90 pounds sterling
Property: All the 300 acre tract called "Bealls Benevolence" in Calvert Co. on the west side of the western branch of the Patuxent River, bounding on "Vail of Benjamin" and land of ALEXANDER MAGRUDER, being land originally granted to EDWARD BOTELER on 1 June 1685 as surveyed on 8 July 1683.
Signature: EDWARD BOTELER
Wit.: JOHN WIGHT, JAMES STODDART
Ackn'd: EDWARD BOTELER and wife ANN, 28 February 1700.
Recorded: 11 July 1701, Vol. A, p. 396

Deed, 13 August 1701
From: MAREEN DUVALL of P. G. Co. and wife FFRANCIS
To: JOHN BARRETT of P. G. Co., gent.
Price: Natural love and affection for their son, MAREEN.
Property: Part of the 1000 acre tract called "Vale of Benjamin" whereon said MAREEN [father or son?] now liveth; conveyance conditional in that FFRANCIS and MAREEN the son shall hold, use, occupy, possess, and enjoy said property during their lives.
Signatures: MAREEN DEVALL, FFRANCIS DEVALL
Wit.: ROBERT TYLER, THOMAS SPRIGG
Ackn'd: MAREEN DUVALL and wife FRANCIS (date of acknowledgement unspecified).
Recorded: 15 August 1701, Vol. A, p. 398

Deed, 26 August 1701
From: Col. HENRY DARNALL of P. G. Co., gent.
To: JOHN MILLER of P. G. Co., planter
Price: 65 pounds sterling
Property: A 200 acre tract consisting of parts of "Timberly" and "Generals Guift" in P. G. Co. on the west side of the Patuxent River in the woods, both the above named tracts having been formerly laid out for ROBERT RIDGLY.
Signature: HENRY DARNALL
Wit.: CLEMMENT HILL, JR., CHARLES BEEKWITH
Ackn'd: HENRY DARNALL, 26 August 1701
Recorded: 4 September 1701, Vol. A, p. 399

Lease, 23 June 1701
From: JOHN LASHLEY of P. G. Co.
To: THOMAS HOLLYDAY of P. G. Co.
Price: Valuable consideration
Property: One house on said LASHLEY'S land commonly
known as "Lashleys Rouleing House," and adjoining
land to make 60 square feet; to hold until Feast of
St. Michael next for 21 years, then for another 21
years, etc., until the world's end; said HOLLYDAY
paying rent of 2 shillings for each 21 year period
on demand.
Signature: JOHN LASHLEY (mark)
Wit.: JOHN BROWNE, JONATHAN SIMONS, JOHN PARNHAM,
and JAMES MULLIKEN (mark).
Ackn'd: "In open court," (date unspecified)
Recorded: 28 October 1701, Vol. A, p. 401

Deed, 8 July 1701
From: ROBERT ANDERSON of P. G. Co., planter
To: RICHARD LANCASTER, late of P. G. Co., merchant
Price: 100 pounds sterling
Property: A 207 acre tract called "New Castle" be-
ing part of a larger tract called "Essington,"
bounding on "Essington," and on land of JOSEPH WIL-
LIAMS.
Signature: ROBERT ANDERSON (mark)
Wit.: ROBERT TYLER, THOMAS SPRIGG, JR.
Ackn'd: ROBERT ANDERSON (mark), and wife ELIZABETH,
8 July 1701.
Recorded: 12 September [sic] 1701, Vol. A, p. 402

Deed, 4 October 1701
From: JOHN ACCATAMACCA, "Empour" of Piscattaway
To: Col. JOHN ADDISON and WILLIAM HUTCHISON, both
of P. G. Co.
Price: 150 arms length of "Roeanoake"
Property: A tract of land on Mattawoman Branch be-
tween the upper road that passes by THOMAS FREDE-
RICK'S down to an Indian path that goes from Maj.
DENT'S Quarter where MATTHEW HINDE formerly lived,
to Accaceeke, not extending back from said Matta-
woman Branch above half a mile.
Signature: "The Emporer" (mark)
Wit.: JOHN BALLDWIN, PHILLIP LE(V?)IN (mark)
Ackn'd: By "The Emporer," 4 October 1701
Recorded: (date unspecified), Vol. A, p. 404

Deed, 27 October 1701
From: JOHN LASHLEY of P. G. Co., planter
To: WILLIAM GREENUP of P. G. Co., planter
Price: 50 pounds sterling
Property: A 100 acre tract called "Cumberland" in
P. G. Co. on the east side of Collington Run, being
part of a tract called "Cobreths Lott," bounding
on "Cobreths Lott," Little Branch, and "Thorpland"
or "Bear Garden," now in the possession of JOHN
BROWNE.
Signature: JOHN LASHLEY (mark)
Wit.: SAMUEL MAGRUDER, SIMON NICHOLLS (mark)
Ackn'd: JOHN LASHLEY, 28 October 1701
Recorded: 10 November 1701, Vol. A, p. 404

Deed, 28 October 1701
From: JOHN LASHLEY of P. G. Co.
To: WM. GASKIN of P. G. Co., planter
Price: 2500 lbs. tobacco
Property: All the 500 acre tract "Gaskins Lott" in
P. G. Co. on the east side of a branch joining Col-
lington Branch called Little Branch, being part of
a larger tract formerly called "Colbreths Lott."
Signature: JOHN LASHLEY (mark)
Wit.: WM. GREENUP, NICHO. BAKER
Ackn'd: JOHN LASHLEY, 28 October 1701
Recorded: 11 October [sic] 1701, Vol. A, p. 406

Deed, 24 September 1700
From: ROBERT TYLER of P. G. Co., gent.
To: SAMUELL FARMER of Anne Arundel Co., planter
Price: 40 pounds sterling
Property: A 103 and 1/4 acre tract called "Farmers
Marsh" in P. G. Co. on the west side of Collington
Branch, being part of a larger tract called "Dar-
nalls Grove," bounded on "Darnalls Grove" and a part
of "Darnalls Grove," now belonging to Mr. ROBERT
BRADLEY.
Signature: ROBERT TYLER
Wit.: WILLIAM TANYHILL, JOSIAS TOWGOOD, RICH'D
DUCKETT.
Ackn'd: ROBERT TYLER and wife SUSANNA, 24 September
1700.
Recorded: 29 November 1701, Vol. A, p. 408

Deed, 19 September 1700
From: JOHN WHEELER of Charles Co., planter, and
wife DORATHY.
To: RICHARD EDGAR of Charles Co.
Price: 6000 lbs. tobacco and 10 shillings
Property: A 200 acre part of "Whelers Purchase" in
P. G. Co. on the east side of Piscattaway River at
an Indian town called Pamunkey, at St. Johns Creek;
said land being part of 500 acres granted to JOHN
WHEELER grandfather of the said JOHN WHEELER afore-
said and bequeathed to him in his grandfather's
will.
Signatures: JOHN WHEELER (mark), DORATHY WHEELER,
(her mark).
Wit.: DAVID HUGHS (mark), DORA GRAVES (mark)
Ackn'd: JOHN WHEELER and wife DORATHY, 19 September
1700.
Recorded: 6 February 1701, Vol. A, p. 411

Quit Claim Deed, 11 September 1700
From: JOHN ACKATAMAKA, "Emporer" of Piscattaway in
the Province of Maryland.
To: JOHN FFENDALL and JOSHUA MARSHALL both of
Charles Co.
Price: 3000 lbs. tobacco
Property: All right and title to an 860 acre tract
lately purchased by them from RANDO HINSON to whom
the tract had originally been granted by Lord Balti-
more.
Signature: "The Emporer" (mark)
Wit.: WILLIAM HUTCHISON, JOHN HAWKINS
Ackn'd: By "Emporer" of Piscattaway, 11 September
1700.
Recorded: 6 February 1701, Vol. A, p. 413

99 Year Lease, 27 October 1701
From: WILLIAM MILLS of P. G. Co.
To: SAMUELL COAPELAND, JOSEPH COPELAND, and HANNA
COAPLAND.
Price: Valuable consideration paid by SAMUELL COPE-
LAND deceased father of the above named SAMUELL,
JOSEPH, and HANNAH COPELAND, and yearly rent of one
ear of Indian corn paid yearly on New Year's Day.
Property: All the 16 acre tract called "Dunbar"
on the north side of Keverns Creek, bounding on

"Coxes Hayes"; to have and hold said land until the
Feast of Annunciation of our Blessed Virgin Mary
next ensuing and thereafter for 99 years.
Signature: WILLIAM MILLS (mark)
Wit.: THOMAS GREENFEILD, MARGRETT SHERDEMOLER (her
mark).
Ackn'd: WILLIAM MILLS, 28 October 1701
Recorded: 6 February 1701, Vol. A, p. 414

Deed, 29 January 1700
From: WILLIAM JONES of P. G. Co., collar maker
To: BEN. BRASSHEERS of P. G. Co., planter
Price: 130 pounds sterling
Property: All the 170 acre tract called "Cuckholds
Delight" in P. G. Co. on the north branch of Patux-
ent River, bounding on FENDALL'S land, "Dunkell,"
and"Moores Plaines."
Signature: WILLIAM JONES (mark)
Wit.: WM. HOLLYDAY, SAMUELL BRASHEAR
Ackn'd: WILLIAM JONES and wife DORATHY, 4 February
1700.
Recorded: 17 February 1701, Vol. A, p. 415

Deed, 29 October 1701
From: THOMAS BROOK of P. G. Co., Esq.
To: Capt. SAMUEL PACY of Kingdom of England,
mariner.
Price: 9000 lbs. tobacco paid, or secured to be
paid, by THOMAS SMITH of Calvert Co., gent., to
THO'S BROOK.
Property: A 100 acre tract not yet surveyed, on
the south side of Mattapony Creek in the freshes
of Patuxent River, bounding on land of Maj. NICHOLAS
SAWELL, and ROBERT ORME, being part of "Brookefeild."
Signature: THOMAS BROOKE
Wit.: R. BRADLEY, JAMES STODDART
Ackn'd: THOMAS BROOKE and wife BARBARY, 29 October
1701.
Recorded: 18 February 1701, Vol. A, p. 417

Deed, 22 August 1700
From: JAMES CONNOWAY of the parish of Stepney Alms,
Stebnnheath, County of Middlesex, mariner, one of
the Executors of the last will and testament of

JOHN MEEKES, late of the parish of St. Pauls, Shad-
well, County of Middlesex, Chyrurgion, deceased;
ARCHIBALD ARTHUR of the parish of St. Margretts,
Pattents, Chyrurgion, and ANN his wife, and SARAH
HELME of the parish of Wapping, While Chappel, County
of Middlesex, widow, the other Executor of the last
will of the said JOHN MEEKES.
To: THOMAS ADDISON of P. G. Co., merchant
Price: 40 pounds sterling
Property: A 400 acre tract called "Chichester" on
the east side of Anocustin River and on the south
side of Isodoras Creek. Said land was bequeathed to
JAMES CONNAWAY in the will of JOHN MEEKES dated 11
July 1691, with instruction to sell the land and pay
the receipts to said MEEKES' son BENJAMIN MEEKES and
his daughter SARAH HELME, with the stipulation that
if the son died without issue before receiving the
legacy, then the receipts were to be divided equally
between MEEKES' daughter SARAH HELME and ANN ARTHUR,
and the said son did die intestate and without issue.
Signatures: JAMES CONNOWAY, ARCHIBALLD ARTHER, ANN
ARTHER, and SARAH HELME.
Wit.: SAM'LL MASON, JO. MASON, WM. SMITH
Ackn'd: By all the grantees, 31 August 1700, at
London, England.
Recorded: 21 February 1701, Vol. A, p. 419

999 Year Lease, 1 September 1701
From: DAVID SMALL of P. G. Co., merchant
To: THOMAS EMMS of the City of London, mariner
Price: 35,000 lbs. tobacco and yearly rent of one
grain of Indian corn each October 10th.
Property: All the 250 acre tract "Kingsaile" for-
merly in Calvert Co., now in P. G. Co., on the west
side of the dividing creek of Patuxent River, and
on St. Charles Branch, bounding on land of CHARLES
BROOKE, and on THOMAS TRYMAN'S (also spelled TRUMAN)
"Deer Bought." Said land was originally patented to
JOHN HUMES of Calvert Co., planter, who conveyed the
land to DAVID SMALL, 21 September 1694.
Signature: DAVID SMALL
Wit.: JAMES STODDERT, EDWARD BATTSON
Ackn'd: DAVID SMALL, 25 November 1701
Recorded: 23 February 1701, Vol. A, p. 424

Deed, 26 April 1700
From: ROBERT SOLLARS of Calvert Co., planter, and
wife MARY.
To: RICHARD JONES of P. G. Co., planter
Price: 80 pounds sterling
Property: All the 100 acre tract "Bealington" and
all the 100 acre tract "Good Luck," both originally
in Calvert Co. on the west side of Patuxent River
and on the west side of the dividing creek or western branch of Patuxent River. "Bealington" was
originally granted to NINIAN BEALE of Calvert Co.,
1 May 1672, and bounded on WILLIAM GROOME'S "Groome
Lott," and on "Good Luck." The land was conveyed
by BEALE to WILLIAM SELLBY, 15 May 1693. "Good
Luck" was originally granted to ALLEXANDER MAGRUDER
of Calvert Co., 1 May 1672, and by him bequeathed
to his son SAMUELL MAGRUDER. SAMUELL MAGRUDER sold
the land to WILLIAM SELLBY of Calvert Co., planter,
14 March 1683, for which there is a confirmatory
deed dated 3 October 1700. WILLIAM SELLBY bequeathed both parcels of land to his son-in-law
ROBERT SOLLARS and his wife MARY in his will dated
5 November 1698.
Signatures: ROBERT SOLLARS, MARY SOLLARS
Wit.: ROBT. BRADLEY, SAM'LL MAGRUDER
Ackn'd: ROBERT SOLLARS and wife MARY, 26 April 1701
Recorded: 27 February 1701, Vol. A, p. 427

Deed, 6 February 1701
From: THOMAS LEMARR of P. G. Co., planter
To: JOHN POTTINGER of P. G. Co., planter
Price: 40 pounds sterling
Property: The 100 acre tract "Samuels Delight" on
Collington Branch, bounding on "Majors Lott" and
Maj. SEWELL'S "Bachilors Hope"; being part of a
larger tract called "Batchelors Delight."
Signature: THOMAS LEMARR
Wit.: SAMEL MAGRUDER, THOMAS SPRIGG, JR., JONATHAN
SIMMONS.
Ackn'd: THOMAS LEMARR and wife ANN, 6 February 1701
Recorded: 5 May 1702, Vol. A, p. 432

Deed, 14 March 1701
From: JOHN CHAPMAN of P. G. Co., planter
To: WILLIAM HOLLYDAY of P. G. Co., gent.

Price: 12,000 lbs. tobacco
Property: The 365 acre tract "Bower" in P. G. Co.,
which was surveyed 15 December 1698, being part of
the surplus lands in the 600 acre tract called
"Churtsey" which was granted to JOHN CHAPMAN, 25
May 1700.
Signature: JOHN CHAPMAN
Wit.: THOMAS HOLLYDAY, JAMES STODDART
Ackn'd: JOHN CHAPMAN and wife ALCE, 14 March 1701
Recorded: 7 May 1702, Vol. A, p. 434

Deed, 18 April 1702
From: RICHARD JONES of P. G. Co., planter
To: EDWARD WILLETT of P. G. Co., pewterer
Price: 50 pounds sterling
Property: All the 100 acre tract "Bealington" in
P. G. Co. on the west side of Dividing Creek of the
Patuxent River, bounding on WILLIAM GROOME'S tract
"Groome Lott," and on "Good Luck."
Signature: RICHARD JONES (mark)
Wit.: ROBERT BRADLEY, JAMES STODDERT
Ackn'd: RICHARD JONES and wife ANNE, 18 April 1702
Recorded: 7 May 1702, Vol. A, p. 437

Mortgage, 15 September 1694
From: NICHOLAS TERRETT of Anne Arundel Co., cooper
To: JOHN BARRETT of Calvert Co., planter
Price: 107 pounds sterling and 10 shillings paid,
or to be paid to THOMAS HILLARY of Calvert Co.
Property: The 150 acre northwest half of "Maw-
burnes Plaines" in Calvert Co. on the south side
of Western Branch or Dividing Creek of Patuxent
River in the freshes, bounding on Cabin Branch.
This deed to be null and void if said TERRETT pays
said BARRETT 215 pounds sterling according to a
note dated 15 September 1694.
Signature: NICHOLAS TERRETT
Wit.: THOMAS HOLLYDAY, EDWARD WILLETT
Ackn'd: NICHOLAS TERRETT and wife JANE, 15 Septem-
ber 1694.
Recorded: 16 June 1702, Vol. A, p. 440

Deed, 28 November 1699
From: THOMAS STOCKETT of Anne Arundel Co., gent.,
Executor of the last will and testament of MARY YATE,

late of Anne Arundel Co., deceased, widow.
To: JOHN BARRETT of P. G. Co., planter
Price: 29 pounds sterling and 12 shillings
Property: A 148 acre part of "Vale of Benjamin,"
bounding on SAMUELL MAGRUDER'S "Alexandria," and
on Turkey Branch.
Signature: (none)
Wit.: ROBERT TYLER, JAMES STODDART
Ackn'd: THOMAS STOCKETT, 28 November 1699
Recorded: 16 June 1702, Vol. A, p. 443

Transfer of Funds, 24 June 1702
From: Maj. WILLIAM BARTON of P. G. Co., late Sheriff
To: Maj. JOSIAS WILLSON of P. G. Co., now High Sher-
iff.
Property: List of fees collected, primarily tobacco
Signature: WM. BARTON
Wit.: THOMAS TANEY, JOSH.CECELL, WM. STONE
Recorded: (no date specified), Vol. A, p. 445

Deed, 14 March 1701
From: BENJAMIN BRASHEAR of P. G. Co., planter
To: SAMUELL BRASSHEER of P. G. Co., planter
Price: 65 pounds sterling
Property: A 78 acre part of "Cuckholds Delight" in
P. G. Co., bounding on FENDELL'S land.
Signature: BENJAMIN BRASHEAR
Wit.: CLEM'T HILL, JR., WM. LEE
Ackn'd: BENJAMIN BRASHEAR and wife MARY, 14 March
1701.
Recorded: 29 June 1702, Vol. A, p. 445

Deed, 3 June 1702
From: HUGH RILEY of P. G. Co., planter
To: SAMUELL BRASHEAR of P. G. Co., planter
Price: 39 pounds sterling
Property: The 60 acre tract, "The ___leapenig(?)"
in P. G. Co., bounding on "Cuckholds Delight" and on
FENDELL'S land.
Signature: HUGH RYLEY
Wit.: ROBERT TYLER, THO. SPRIGG, JR.
Ackn'd: HUGH RYLEY and wife MARY, 3 June 1702
Recorded: 29 June 1702, Vol. A, p. 447

Deed, 10 April 1702
From: JAMES NEALE of Charles Co., gent., and wife
ELIZABETH.
To: CHARLES EGARTON of St. Mary's Co., gent.
Price: 5 shillings and consideration of the agree-
ment made between JAMES NEALE and JAMES [CHARLES]
EGARTON prior to the marriage of CHARLES EGARTON
and MARY NEALE, daughter of the said JAMES NEALE.
Property: A 600 acre tract on Piscattaway River
bounding on land of RANDOLPH FENTON and on Indian
field [much of the description covered by an ink
blot]. Said land was part of 3000 acres granted to
WILLIAM CALVERT, Esq., deceased, 11 February 1662.
Said 600 acre tract was given by WILLIAM CALVERT to
his daughter ELIZABETH at her marriage to JAMES
NEALE, and was excluded from the conveyance whereby
CHARLES CALVERT, son and heir of said WILLIAM CAL-
VERT, deceased, conveyed title to 2400 acres of the
tract to CHARLES EGARTON, deceased father of the
CHARLES EGARTON who was a party to these presents.
Signatures: JAMES NEALE, ELIZ'A NEALE (mark)
Wit.: ANTHO'Y NEALE, CHARLES DIGGES
Ackn'd: JAMES NEALE and wife ELIZABETH, 18 April
1702.
Recorded: 1 July 1702, Vol. A, p. 449

Deed, 28 April 1701
From: PETER JOY of St. Mary's Co., planter, and
wife ANNE.
To: Col. HENRY DARNALL of P. G. Co.
Price: 100 pounds sterling
Property: The 250 acre tract called "Kingstone" in
P. G. Co., formerly in Calvert Co., on the west side
of Patuxent River, in the woods about two miles
from Dividing Creek.
Signatures: PETER JOY (mark), ANNE JOY (mark)
Wit.: JOHN NUTTHALL, RICH'D BUTHORON
Ackn'd: PETER JOY and wife ANNE, 3 May 1701
Recorded: 3 June 1702, Vol. A, p. 451

PRINCE GEORGE'S COUNTY

- - PRESENT BOUNDARY
TRACT KEY: PAGES 80-82

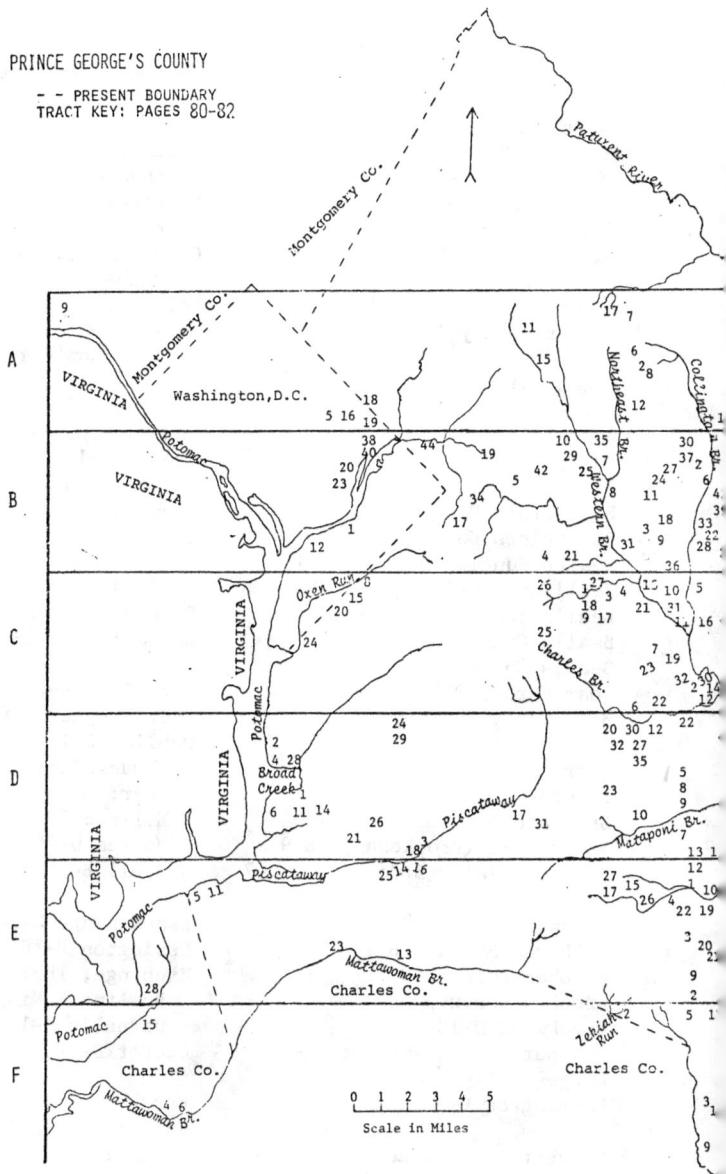

Patuxent River

Montgomery Co.

A

VIRGINIA

Montgomery Co.

Washington, D.C.

9

11
15
18
5 16 19

17 7
6
2 8
12

Collington

Northeast Br.

B

VIRGINIA

Potomac

38 40
20
23
44
19
34
17
5 42

10 35
29 7
2
8
4 21
31

30
27 37 2
24
11
3 18
9
26

6
4
33
22
28

1
12

Western Br.

C

VIRGINIA

Potomac

Oxen Run
15
20
24

26
18
9 17
25
23

12
3 4
21
7 19
6 22

13 10 5
31
11 16
32 2
12

Charles Br.

D

VIRGINIA

Potomac

Broad Creek

2
4 28
6 11 14
24
29
26
21
18
17 31

Piscataway

20 30 12
32 27
35
23
10

22
5
8
9

Mataponi Br.

13 1

E

VIRGINIA

Potomac

5 11
Piscataway
25 14 16
27 15
17
26

12
1 10
22 19

3 20
2
9
2

23
13
Mattawoman Br.
Charles Co.

5 1

28
15

F

Potomac

Charles Co.

Mattawoman Br.
4 6

Zekiah Run 2

Charles Co.

3

9

0 1 2 3 4 5
Scale in Miles

MAP TRACT KEY

Aaron B-1
Acquascat F-1
Addisons Expidition D-1
Addition E-1
Admirothona D-2
Alexandria C-1
Amptill Grange A-1
Anchovis Hill E-2
Apple Hill D-3
Archers Pasture E-3
Arthers Folly (Stoney Hill) D-4

Bacon Hall C-2
Balls Good Luck D-5
Barrens E-4
Bartons Hope F-2
Batchelors Delight A-2; B-37
Batchelors Harbour D-6
Batchelors Hope B-2
Beales Hunting Quarter B-3
Bealington C-3
Bealls Benevolence B-4
Bealls Craft C-4
Bealls Guift B-5
Bear Garden C-5
Beginning, The B-6
Berry Fortune C-6
Berry Lott B-7
Bower*
Bred and Cheese B-8
Brock Hall (Brookehall) B-9
Brookes Field (Brookfield) D-7
Brookes Grove:
  Baker Brookes C-7
  Thomas Brookes B-10
Brookes Point D-8
Brookes Reserve D-9
Brookwood D-10
Brothers Joynt Interest C-8
Burges Delight*
Buttington F-3

Calvert Manor (See Mount Cal-
  vert Manor & Charles Town)
Cattail Meadows A-3
Charighigth [Creighnight?] C-9

Charles Town (Mount Calvert)
  C-28
Charley E-5
Chelsey (Chesley) B-11
Chichester B-12
Churtsey*
Clarkes Purchase F-4
Clarksons Purchase D-11
Cobreths Lott C-10
Cold Spring Manor B-13
Collington C-11
Collins Comfort E-6
Compass Hills F-5
Concord A-4
Coxes Hayes E-7
Croome D-12
Croscloth D-13
Crouches Guift F-6
Cuckholds Delight:
  [1] B-14
  [2] A-5
Cuckholds Poynt C-12
Cumberland C-13

Darnalls Grove A-6
Dear Bought C-14
Dubling D-14
Duchmans Imployment A-7
Dunbar:
  Mills F-7
  Moores D-15
Dunkell B-15

Essex Lodge D-16
Essington B-16
Exchange, The:
  Bowling & Kings E-8
  Darnalls D-17
Exeter D-18

Farme, The D-19
Farmers Marsh A-8
Fendalls Spring B-13
First Late [Lot?] B-6
Forrest, The:
  Thomas Brookes D-31

80

* Indicates insufficient bounds given within these deeds to collaborate general location of tract.

INDEX

83

"Batchelors Hope," 19, 75.
BATSON (Battson), Edward, 16,
    20, 55, 56, 57, 58-59,
    74.
BATTIE (Bate, Batte),
    John, 12, 57, 58.
BAYLEY, William, 22.
"Beales Hunting Quarter,"
    11.
"Bealington," 75, 76.
BEALL, James, 37, 44.
    Col. Ninian, 1, (sheriff)
    6, 7, 10, 11, 12, 15, 16,
    19, 28, 33, 34, 37, 38,
    48, 49, 53, 54, 55, (Maj.)
    59, 66, 75.
    Ruth, 11, 15, 16, 33, 34,
    37, 38, 49, 54, 55, 66.
"Bealls Benevolence," 69.
"Bealls Craft," 33, 65.
"Bealls Guift," 66.
BEANES (Bains, Banes, Beans),
    Christopher, 13, 26, 34,
    57.
"Bear Garden," 71.
BEATTY (See BATTIE).
Beaver Dam Branch, 53, 56,
    64.
BEDGEET, Thomas, 13.
BEEKWITH, Charles, 69.
BEGGER (See BIGGER).
"Beginning, The," 13, 24,
    25, 26.
BELL, James, 63.
    Sarah Pearce, 63.
    Thom., 30.
BELT (Bellt), Elizabeth, 53,
    64, 65.
    John, 64.
    Joseph, 64.
BENNETT, Rob., 25.
BENTON, Rich'd, 27.
BERRY, Benjamin, 7, 33, 39,
    48, 52, 59.
    James, 10, 30.
    Mary, 48.
    Nehmiah, 10.

BERRY (continued),
    William, 10.
"Berry Fortune," 40.
"Berry Lott," 48.
BIGGER(S) (Begger, Biggars),
    James, 3, 4, 16.
    John, 11, 15, 16, 18, 54.
    Col. John, 65.
    Walter, 15, 16.
BIGGS, John, 41.
BILLINGER, Ellinor, 2.
    Francis, 2.
BIRD, Jno., 29, 48.
Blacksmith (See Occupation).
BLAY, Edward, 45.
BOAGUE, Jno., 23.
BOND, Abell, 40.
BONNER, Henry, 34, 56.
BOTELER (See also BUTLER),
    Ann, 69.
    Edward, 68, 69.
BOULTON, James, 4.
BOWDELLS, Thomas, 6.
"Bower," 76.
BOWLING, John, 39, 55, 56.
    Mary, 56.
    Thomas, 12.
BOX, Thomas, 34, 65.
BOYD(E), John, 14, 15, 17,
    19, 41.
    Jn'a., 40.
    Mary, 15, 17.
BOYNE, John, 53.
BRADLEY (Bradly), Mr., 31,
    57.
    R., 49, 60, 73.
    Robert, 32, 41, 47, 59,
    61, 62, 63, 64, 65, 68,
    71, 75, 76.
BRAN, George, 8.
BRASHEAR (Brassheer, Breashear),
    Benjamin, 68, 73, 77.
    Mary, 77.
    Samuell, 73, 77.
BRATT, Thomas (alias Thomas
    Bridges), 55.
"Bred and Cheese," 33.

BRENT, George, 54.
  George Jun'r, 8.
  Nicholas, 54.
Bridge Branch, 47.
BRIDGES (See BRATT, Thomas).
BRIGHTWELL, Capt. Richard, 15.
Broad Creek, 14, 43, 50, 67.
BROCK (Broch), Capt., 11, 46.
"Brock Hall (Brookehall)," 44,
  68.
BROCKDEN, Richard, 17.
BROOKE(S) (Brooks),
  Bakers, 11.
  Barbara, 45, 47, 64, 73.
  Charles, 25, 37, 51, 54, 74.
  Clement, 19.
  James, 40.
  Robert, 10, 18, 19, 40.
  Roger, 9, 29, 40.
  Roger Jr., 17.
  Thomas, 8, 12, 18, 19, 22,
    23, 32, 45, 46, 47, 63,
    64, 73.
  Maj. Thomas, 11, 19, 60.
Brookes Creek, 8.
  Branch of, 8, 46.
"Brookes Field (Brookfield),"
  8, 18, 19, 46, 47, 73.
"Brooke(s) Grove,"
  Baker Brookes' (bounds on
    "Bacon Hall"), 11.
  Thomas Brookes' (bounds on
    "Northampton"), 45.
"Brookes Point," 29, 40.
"Brooks Reserve," 40.
"Brookhall" (See "Brock Hall").
"Brookwood," 32.
BROTHERS, Mary, 24.
  Nathaniel, 13, 24.
"Brothers Joynt Interest," 2.
BROWEN, John, 24.
BROWN(E), John, 1, 2, 35, 41,
  70, 71.
  Joseph, 52, 60.
BROYN, John, 19.
BURGES (Burgis), George, 31,
  40.

BURGES (continued),
  Katherine, 31.
  Peter, 6.
"Burges Delight," 31.
BUTHORON, Rich'd, 78.
BUTLER (Buttler), (See also
  BOTELER),
  Charles, 25, 40, 51.
  James, 36.
BUTT, Richard, 61.
"Buttington," 53.
BYRD (See BIRD).

Cabin Branch, 34, 45, 65, 76.
CALVERT, Cecilius (Lord
    Proprietor), 3.
  Charles, 78.
  Charles (Lord Baltimore),
    1, 6.
  Elizabeth (Neale), 78.
  Phillip, 13, 31, 33, 34,
    57.
  William, 78.
"Calvert Manor," 57. (See
  also "Mount Calvert
  Manor").
Calverts Branch, 13, 31, 57.
CAMELL, Patrick, 3.
Canadoyes Branch, 10.
CARLETON, Augus., 3, 4.
Carpenter (See Occupation).
CARROLL, Charles, 9, 25, 37,
  54, 66.
CARTWRIGHT, Demetrius, 17.
CARVILLE, Robert, 25, 28.
CASH, John, 23, 35.
Cattail Marsh, 35, 41.
"Cattail Meadows," 17.
CECELL (Cecill), Joshua, 14,
  18, 20, 21, 24, 25, 26,
  29, 36, 48, 56, 64, 77.
Cecilius (See CALVERT).
CHAFFEE, Richard, 21.
CHAIRES, Jno., 27.
CHANDLER, William, 50.
Chaplico Branch, (See
  Chaptico Branch).

CHAPMAN, Alce, 76.
John, 75, 76.
Chaptico (Chaplico) Branch,
In St. Mary's Co., 3.
"Charighigth" ["Creighnight"?],
66. (See also "Magruders
Delight").
Charles, Lord Baltimore, (See
CALVERT).
Charles (St. Charles) Branch,
25, 40, 46, 51, 74.
Charlestown (P. G. Co.), 13,
15, 20, 24, 25, 31, (Act
of Assembly creating) 57.
CHARLETT, Rich., 15.
"Charley," 5.
"Chelsey (Chesley)," 11, 20,
21.
CHEW, Benjamin, 44.
Joseph, 59.
"Chichester," 74.
CHITTAM, Ann, 39.
John, 2, 7, 39, 41.
Church (See St. Paul's).
"Churtsey," 76.
CLAGGETT (Clegget),
Thomas, 51.
CLARK(E), Abraham, 32.
Benjamin, 49, 50, 51, 52.
Daniel, 31.
Elizabeth, 50, 52.
Francis, 49, 50, 51, 52.
John, 49, 50, 51, 52.
Judith, 50, 52.
Phillip, 26, 27, 28.
Richard, 5, 68.
Robert, 43, 49, 50, 51, 52.
William, 56.
"Clarkes Purchase," 49.
CLARKSON, Ruth, 43, 50.
William, 14, 43, 50, 65.
"Clarksons Purchase," 43.
Clash [Clark?] Creek, 43.
CLEGGETT (See CLAGGETT).
Cliffs, The, (Calvert Co.) 44.
CLULK, Jacob, 45.
COARTS, COATS, (See COURTS).

"Cobreths Lott," 71.
"Cold Spring Manor," 30, 37.
Collar Maker (See Occupation).
COLLINGS (Collins), Ann, 32.
George, 18, 19, 55.
William, 32, 55, 61.
"Collington," 52.
Collington Branch, 6, 13, 17,
24, 25, 26, 41, 60, 71,
75.
East side of, 8.
Head of, 38, 39.
North side of, 17.
Southwest side of, 11.
West side of, 15, 47, 59,
61, 63, 71.
Collington Run, 71.
"Collins Comfort," 32, 55.
COLLYER (Colliar),
Francis, 30, 41.
"Compass Hills," 23, 66.
COMPTEN, James, 14.
"Concord," 17.
CONNOWAY, James, 73, 74.
COOD, Col. John, 27.
COOKE, Charles, 45.
COOPE, George, 8.
Cooper (See Occupation).
COPELAND (Coapland),
Hanna, 72.
Joseph, 72.
Samuell, 72.
Cornelius Branch, 10.
COURTS (Coarts, Coats),
John, 52.
Courts, County, 26, 27.
Provincial, 26, 27, 28,
41.
COUSENS (Cousons), John, 46.
"Coxes Hayes," 73.
CRABB, Thomas, 48.
CRANFORD, James, 10.
CRAYCROFT (Creycroft),
Ignatius, 10, 18, 19.
John, 10.
"Croome," 16, 25, 51, 54.
"Croscloth," 19.

"Crouches Guift," 52.
CRUNWYN, Thomas, 25.
CRYER, John, 22.
"Cuckholds Delight":
  Between Collington & North
    Branches, 6, 60, 73, 77.
  On Eastern Branch, 58, 68.
"Cuckholds Poynt," 36.
CULLEN, James, 25.
CULVER, Henry, 9, 40.
"Cumberland," 71.

DANNISONE, Daniel Jr., 7.
  Daniel Sr., 7.
DARNALL, Elinor, 50, 51.
  Col. Henry, 6, 9, 18, 25,
    37, 38, 50, 51, 54, 64,
    69, 78.
  John, 19, 41.
  Phillip, 19.
"Darnalls Grove," 15, 47, 59,
    61, 63, 68, 71.
DAVES, William, 9.
DAVIS (Davice),
  Elizabeth, 36.
  John, 13, 20, 24, 25, 26,
    36, 57.
  Honnor, 1, 2.
  Nicholas, 23.
  Thomas, 1, 2.
DEAKINS, John, 26, 28.
"Dear Bought," 36, 74.
Deep Creek, 22, 32, 39, 40,
    55, 56, 60.
  Head of, 39, 55.
  South main branch, 60.
Deep Gully Branch, 39.
DEMALL, John, 11, 25, 26, 45,
    (John's Back Branch) 46.
  Mary, 46.
DENT, Elizabeth, 5.
  George, 2.
  Maj., 70.
  Peter, 5.
  William, 2, 3, 5.
DEVALL (See DUVALL).

DIGGES, Charles, 78.
Dividing Creek (See Patuxent
    River).
DODSON, John, 49.
DRAINE (Drayne, Dreine),
  Anthony, 39, 45.
"Dubling," 34.
"Duchmans Imployment," 38.
DUCKETT, Richard, 61, 71.
"Dunbar":
  Wm. Mill's (bounding on
    "Coxes Hayes"), 72.
  James Moore's (bounding
    on "Essex Lodge"), 64.
"Dunkell," 1, 73.
DURHAM, Alice, 44.
  Richard, 44, 68.
DUVALL (Devall),
  Francis, 69.
  Lewis, 61.
  Mareen, 1, 9, 41, 69.
  Samuel, 61.

Eastern Branch (See Potomac
    River).
EDELIN, Richard, 43, 52, 54.
EDGAR, Richard, 72.
EDMUNSON (Edmonston,
    Edmundson),
  Archibald, 2, 32, 48, 49,
    55.
  Thomas, 15, 19.
EDWARDS, Hannah Potts, 2,
    30, 40.
  John, 40.
  Richard, 2, 30, 37.
EGARTON, Charles, 78.
  James, 78.
  Mary Neale, 78.
ELDERSLEY, Henry, 27.
ELDIN, Will'm, 27.
ELLIOT, William, 14.
EMMET, John, 7.
EMMS (Emes, Emmes),
  Capt. Thomas, 13, 26, 31,
    33, 34, 57, 74.

Emperor of Piscattaway (See
ACCATAMACCA, John).
England, 22, 37, 55, 73, 74.
London, 13, 24, 25, 29, 31,
33, 37, 40, 44, 57, 68,
74, (St. Clemons of) 29.
Middlesex County, 73, 74.
Shadwell (St. Pauls
Parish), 74.
Stebnnheath (Stepney Alms
Parish), 73.
While [White?] Chapel
(Wapping Parish), 74.
"Essex Lodge," 24, 64.
"Essington," 14, 17, 32, 70.
EVANS, Richard, 7, 62.
"Exchange, The":
Bowling & King's (bounds
on "Collins Comfort" &
"Mansfield"), 39, 55, 56.
Darnall's (bounds on Dar-
nall's "The Forest"), 64.
"Exeter," 52.
EYRE, Jane Severne, 16.
Thomas, 16.

FALKNER, Mary Moore, 11.
"Farme, The," 32.
FARMER, Mich'll, 3.
Samuell, 39, 68, 71.
"Farmers Marsh," 71.
FAULKS, Richard, 65.
Fees, tobacco, 77.
FENDALL, Bridgett, 50, 52.
John, 5, 72.
Fendalls Fresh, 30, 37.
Fendalls Land, 2, 30, 73, 77.
"Fendalls Spring," 2, 30.
FENIX (See PHENIX).
FENTON, Randolph, 78.
FENWICK, John, 54.
Ferry, 13, 57.
FINCH, Guy, 9.
Rebecca, 9.
"First Late [Lot?], The," 26.
FITZHERBERT, Maj., 9, 29.

Fordsham Creek (Indiantowne
Creek), 53.
FORREST, Elizabeth, 3.
John, 3.
"Forrest, The":
Thomas Brookes' (bounds on
Darnall's "Exchange"), 64.
John Forrest's (on Chaptico
Branch, in St. Mary's
County), 3.
"Four Hills," 40.
Fransum Creek (See Indian-
towne Creek).
FREDERICK, Thomas, 67, 70.
Freeman, 49.
FREEMAN, Francis, 32.
"Friends Choyce," 64.
"Friendship," 5.
FRY, David, 45.
Edward, 44, 45.
"Frys Choice," 45.

GALE, John, 1, 49.
GALWITH, Jane, 10.
John, 10.
GAMBLIN(G), James, 3, 4.
"Garden, The," 2.
GARDNER (Gardiner,
Gardioner),
John, 19.
Luke, 36.
Margery, 9.
GASKIN, William, 71.
"Gaskins Lott," 71.
GATTON, Tho., 43.
"Gedling," 61.
"Generals Gift," 16, 51, 69.
GETTINGS (Gittings),
Phillip, 45.
"Giants Range," 52.
GIBBENS, Thomas, 12.
GIBSON, John, 44.
GLOVER, Rober., 5.
"Gods Guift," 65.
GOFF, Bartholomew, 42.

"Good Luck":
  Ball's, (100 acres, bounds on Brookes' Point") 29.
  Belt's, (100 acres, bounds on "Three Sisters") 53, 64.
  Edward's, (50 acre part of "Cold Spring Manor") 30.
  Magruder's, (100 acres, bounds on "Bealington") 66, 75, 76.
  Wade's, (445 acre portion, bounds on "Rovers Content") 36, 37.
  Addition to, (200 acres, bounds on Belt's "Good Luck") 53, 64.
GOODERWEEK, Francis Jr., 34.
  Francis Sr., 34.
"Goores, The," 22.
GOSLING, John, 55.
Governor, of Maryland, 27.
  Of Virginia, 26-28.
Grand Jury, 27, 28.
GRAVES, Dora, 72.
GRAY, Sam'll, 27.
GREAR, (See also GREERE)
  John, 10.
GREEN, James, 67.
  John, 31.
  Luke, 8.
  Thomas, 68.
GREENE, Charles, 21, 22.
  Elizabeth Truman, 21, 22.
"Greenfield," 45.
GREENFIELD (Greenfeild),
  James, 61.
  Martha, 22, 23, 61.
  T. Truman (Thomas Truman), 22, 61.
  Thomas, 3, 6, 15, 21, 22, 23, 30, 61, 66, 67, 73.
GREENUP, William, 71.
GREER(E), Joseph, 4, 10, 12.
  Sarah, 12.
GRIFFITH (Griffeth),
  Elizabeth, 37.

GRIFFITH (continued),
  Samuell, 37.
GROOME, Ann, 23, 24.
  Marg't, 30.
  Mary, 13, 14, 20, 26, 31, 34, 57.
  Richard, 13, 20, 23, 24, 31, 47, 48, 49, 57.
  Richard (of London), 29, 30.
  Susan, 30.
  William [Jr.], 13, 14, 20, 24, 26, 31, 34, 57.
  William [Sr.], 13, 31, 34, 57, 75, 76.
"Groome Lott," 75, 76.
"Grove Hurst," 56.
"Grove Landing," 11.

HADDUCK (Haddock),
  Benjamin, 6, 28, 55, 58.
"Hadducks Hill," 28.
"Hales Rest," 46.
HALL, Joshua, 6, 7, 41, 52.
  Margaret, 6.
HALLYDAY (See HOLLYDAY).
HAMBLETON, Andrew, 58.
HAMMOND, John, 27.
HANCE, John, 32.
HANSON (Hansen, Henson, Hinson),
  Barbara, 5.
  Randolph, 5, 72.
"Hansonton," 5.
HARBERT (Herbert),
  Alexander, 43.
  Mary, 65.
  William, 21, 38, 49, 65.
"Hargrove," 19.
HARRIS, Will., 45.
HARRISON, Francis, 36.
  Richard, 40.
HARWOOD, Richard, 40.
HATTON, Thomas, 4, (Secretary of the Province) 10, 12.
  William, 7, 27, 42.
HAWKINS, Elizabeth, 43.

HAWKINS (continued),
John, 16, 25, 35, 42, 43,
54, 66, 67, 72.
Thomas, 48.
"Hazard," 32.
HEAD, William, 16.
HELME, Sarah Meekes, 74.
HENSON (See HANSON).
HERBERT (See HARBERT).
HILL, Clement, 63.
Clement Jr., 19, 54, 69,
77.
Richard, 27.
HILLARY (Hillery),
Elinor (Nutwell), 47, 62.
Thomas, 47, 53, 62, 64, 76.
HILLS, Thomas, 51.
HINDE, Matthew, 70.
HINSON (See HANSON).
"His Lordships Manor" ["Coll-
ington (Calverton) Manor"]
47, 59.
HOBBS, Robert, 27.
HOLDSWORTH, Samuel, 59.
HOLLYDAY (Hallyday),
Col., 33.
Thomas, 7, 13, 15, 24, 28,
29, 33, 37, 47, 59, 65,
66, 70, 76.
William, 12, 73, 75.
HOLMES, Edward, 60, 61.
HONBLON (See MAIJOR).
"Hopewell," 2.
Horse Pen Branch, 38, 39.
"Horse Race, The," 33, 34,
65.
HOSKINS (Hosskins, Hopkins),
Phillip, 27, 50, 52.
HOW, Henry, 3.
"Huckleberry Patch," 1.
HUGGINS, John, 58.
HUGHS, David, 72.
"Hughs Labour," 8.
HUMES, John, 74.
HUNTS (See also TUNKS),
Henry, 23.

HUTCHISON (Hutcheson),
Sarah, 34, 52, 67.
William, 1, 2, 5, 6, 29, 34,
42, 50, 52, 62, 67, 70,
72.
HYATT, Charles, 24.
HYDE, Thomas, 9, 29.

"Inclosure," 37, 55.
Indians:
Emperor (Accatamacca, John),
70, 72.
Field [lands], 65, 78.
Path, 8, 70.
Mattapony Path, 39, 55.
Villages: Accokeek, 5, 70.
Pamunkey, 72.
Piscataway, 70, 72.
"Indian Creeke with Addition,"
21.
"Indian Field," 13.
Indiantowne Creek (Brook),
[Also called Fransum, Ford-
sham, Transum Creek], 4,
10, 12, 53.
Innholder (See Occupation).
ISAAC (Isaack, Isack),
Edward, 6.
Richard, 6, 52, 60, 61.
Isodoras Creek [Also called
Eastern Branch of the
Potomac River], 64.

JACKSON, George, 4.
Thomas, 5.
JACOB, John, 27, 40.
JAMES, Thomas, 35, 53.
"James Gift," 21.
JENKINSON, Daniel, 65.
Jeroms Creek [Also called
Swan Creek], 67.
JOHNS, Richard, 44.
JONES, Anne, 76.
Dorathy, 73.

JONES (continued),
  George, 61.
  Hugh, 64.
  Morg'n, 27.
  Richard, 75, 76.
  William, 73.
JOSEPH, William, 29.
"Jourdan" (in Charles Co.),
  29.
JOWLES, Henry, 7.
  Col. Henry, 56.
  Henry Jr., 56.
  Sible, 56.
JOY, Anne, 78.
  Peter, 11, 78.
JOYCE, John, 6, 30.
  Susanna, 63.
Jurors, 27, 41.
Justices, 26, 27.

KEECH, James, 37, 50, 52.
Kent Co. (Maryland), 44.
"Kettering," 63.
Keverns Creek, 72.
KING, John, 39, 55, 56.
"Kingsaile" ["Kingsdale"],
  74.
"Kingstone," 78.
KLUCK, KLUKE, (See CLULK).

LAMARR (Lemarr), Ann, 75.
  Thomas, 19, 75.
LANCASTER, Richard, 70.
Land Office (St. Mary's
  City), 8.
LANG, Anthony, 31.
"Langley," 43.
LANNUM, John, 2.
LARKIN(G), John, 32.
  Thomas, 11.
LARRIMORE, Edward, 27.
"Laset Thicket" (See "Locust
  Thicket").
LASHLEY, John, 70, 71.
Lashley's Rouleing House, 70.

LEE, William, 37, 40, 77.
LEFEVER, Herman, 66.
LEMAN (Lemon), Hickford, 43,
  52, 54, 66, 67.
LEMAR (See LAMAR).
LEROUNT, John, 24.
LETCHWORTH, Thomas, 2, 30.
LE(V?)IN, Phillip, 70.
LEWELLIN(G), John, 17.
LILE (See LYLE).
LINGAN, Ann, 53.
  George, 38, 53, 60.
  Martha (Wilson), 53.
LINGE, John, 22.
Little Branch, 1, 71.
"Little Ease," 38, 43, 54.
"Little Grove," 60.
LOCKER, Sarah (Talbot), 43.
  Thomas, 43.
"Locust Thicket," 38, 43, 54.
LOMAX, Cleburne (Cleborn), 17,
  29.
"Londee" ("Lundy"), 6, 46, 60.
London (See England).
"Long Looked For," 60.
LORD BALTIMORE (See also
  CALVERT), 25, 72.
Lord Proprietor,
  Cecilius [CALVERT], 3.
LOW, Henry, 38, 56.
  William, 69.
LOWE, John, 2.
LOWTHER, John, (Commander) 37.
Lowther Galley, 37.
LOYD, Morris, 54.
"Lundy" (See "Londee").
LYLE (Lile), Elizabeth, 58.
  Robert, 58.
  Samuel, 68.
  William, 58.
Lyles Branch, 55.
LYNES, Margrett, 67.
  Phillip, 2, 10, 67.
LYONS, Jno., 29.

MACKBEE, Matthew, 60.

"Maddozes Fooly" ["Madducks
  Folly"], 14.
MAGRUDER, Allexander, 9, 26,
  61, 66, 69, 75.
  Ann, 66.
  Nathaniell, 66.
  Samuell, 9, 16, 32, 33, 36,
  66, 71, 75, 77.
"Magruders Delight," 66.
"Maidens Dowry, The," 38.
MAIJOR, John Honblon, 5.
"Majors Lott," 19, 26, 41, 75.
MANNING, John, 36.
  Jos., 36.
"Mansfield," 32.
MARBURY (Marberry),
  Francis, 38, 43, 52, 54.
  Mary, 54.
"Margry," 9.
Mariner (See Occupation).
Marsh Branch, 45.
Marsh, Great sunken, 57.
MARSHALL, Joshua, 5, 38, 72.
MARSHAM, Ann, 47, 59.
  Richard, 6, 8, 15, 16, 47,
  55, 59, 60, 61.
Maryland, Province of, 7,
  21, 72.
  Courts, 26-28.
  Governor of, 27.
  Proprietor (See CALVERT).
  Provincial Assembly, Act
  of, 31.
  Secretary of, 10, 12.
MASH, Gilbert, 14.
MASON, George, 10.
  Jo., 74.
  Sam'll, 74.
Mattapony Branch, 64.
Mattapony Creek, 24,29,55,73.
Mattapony Path (See also
  Indians), 39, 55.
Mattawoman Branch, 67, 70.
Mattawoman Creek, 42, 50.
Mattawoman Main Fresh, 50.
"Mawburnes Plaines"
  ["Marborrows Plaines"?], 76.

MAXEY, John, 22.
"Mazoonscon," 22.
McBEE (See MACKBEE).
McC[illegible], Jno., 27.
MEEK(E)S, Ann (Arther), 74.
  Benjamin, 74.
  John, 74.
  Sarah (Helme), 74.
MELLTON, William, 44, 68.
Merchant (See Occupation).
MERITON (Meryton, Moriton),
  [First name not given,
  John?], 8, 31, 35, 47.
  John, 8, 20, 36.
METHUEN, James, 20.
MIDDLETON, Mary, 52.
  Robert, 14, 43, 52.
MILLER, George, 44, 59, 62.
  John, 32, 69.
MILLS, Elizabeth, 67.
  John, 2, 30.
  William, 67, 72, 73.
Minister (See Occupation).
MIRTH (Murth), John, 3, 4, 16.
MOBBERLY, John, 14.
MOHALL, Tim., 15.
MOOR(E), Hugh, 7.
  James, 11, 39, 40, 44, 64,
  65, 66, 68.
  Mary, 40, 64, 65, 66.
  Mary (Falkner), 11.
  Mordicai, 8.
  William, 11.
"Moores Plaines," 44, 68, 73.
MOORLAND (Moreland, Morland),
  Jacob, 56.
MORIARTE, Daniell, 38.
MORITON (See MERITON).
MORLEY, Elizabeth, 58.
  Griffin, 58.
"Mount Calvert," 13, 15, 31,
  33.
"Mount Calvert Manor" (See
  also "Mount Calvert" &
  Charlestown), 20, 24, 26,
  31, 33, 36, 47, 48, 49,
  57.

"Mount Pleasant," 6, 16, 30, 60.
MULLIKIN(S) (Mulliken),
  James, 19, 20, 21, 68, 70.
  Jane, 20, 21.
  Thomas, 20, 21.
MUNDONE, Locklen, 13.
MURTH (See MIRTH).
"Mussell Shell," 11, 59.

Naturalization, 7.
NEALE, Anth'y, 78.
  Elizabeth Calvert, 78.
  James, 78.
  Mary (Egarton), 78.
"New Castle," 70.
"Newton," 22.
NICHOLLS, Simon, 71.
NICHOLSON, Francis, (Governor of Maryland Province), 27.
NORMANSELL, Thomas, 43.
NORRIS (Noris), Caleb, 42.
  William, 37.
North Branch (See Patuxent River).
"Northampton," 45, 63.
Notting (St. Thomases Creek), 50, 52.
"Nottingham," 22.
NUTTWELL (Nutthall),
  Elinor Hillary, 47, 62.
  John Jr., 47, 62, 78.

Occupations:
  Apothecary, 21.
  Blacksmith, 34, 65.
  Carpenter, 2, 5, 7, 8, 11, 13, 26, 28, 32, 42, 44, 46.
    Tools, 42.
  Collar Maker, 73.
  Cooper, 22, 24, 32, 36, 42, 76.
  Innholder [Innkeeper], 13, 20, 26, 31, 47, 57.

Occupations: (continued)
  Mariner, 13, 24, 31, 33, 35, 37, 55, 57, 73, 74,
  Sailorman, 4.
  Merchant, 7, 8, 13, 24, 31, 33, 39, 40, 44, 47, 48, 57, 68, 74.
    Of London, 37, 40.
  Minister, 15.
  Pewterer, 65, 76.
  Plaisterer [Plasterer], 29.
  Planter, 1-6, 8-14, 17, 19, 20-21, 23-26, 28-33, 35, 36-39, 41-49, 51-56, 58, 60-73, 75-78.
  Sailorman, 4.
  Servant, 39.
  Sheriff, 6, 77.
  Ship Commander, 37.
  Surveyor, 41.
  Tailor, 6, 11, 29, 33, 52, 60.
ODELL, Thomas, 63.
ODEN, Jo., 27.
ORME, Robert, 8, 64, 73.
Oxen Run, 2, 8.
"Oxmontown," 34.

Packletts Meddow Branch, 33.
PACY, Capt. Samuel, 73.
PAGGETT, Sarah, 4, 10.
  Thomas, 4, 10, 12.
PALMAR, Thomas, 3.
Pamankey Neck (of Potomac River), 42.
Pamunkey (See Indians).
PARK(E), Phillip, 27.
  Phillip (of London), 24.
PARNHAM, John, 70.
"Partnership," 41.
Patuxent River, 13, 14, 17, 31.
  Dividing (Fork) of, 11, 13, 20, 24, 26, 31, 34, 57.
  Freshes of, 10, 13, 20, 38, 73.

Patuxent River, (continued)
Dividing Creek, 36, 74, 75,
76, 78.
North Branch of, 2, 6, 16,
17, 46, 60, 73.
North side of, 61.
South side of, 3, 4, 18, 59.
Southwest Branch of, 33, 66.
Southwest side of, 3.
West side of, 6, 9-10, 13,
15-20, 22-26, 30-32, 34,
35-37, 40-41, 45-47, 51,
52-57, 59, 60, 63-64, 69,
75, 78.
Western Branch of, 1, 9, 11,
19, 33-35, 47-49, 53, 59,
62-66, 69, 75, 76.
PEAKE, Jo., 27.
PEARCE, John, 63.
Sarah (Bell), 63.
Sarah (Sprigg), 63.
"Penthen Hills" ["Pintlin
Hills"], 52.
PERRY, Capt. Richard, 11, 35.
"Perry Hills," 35.
PERSONE, Thomas, 14.
PETER, Samuel, 35, 53.
Petition, 15, 26-28.
Pewterer (See Occupation).
PHENIX (Fenix), Edward, 36.
Pig (Pen) Poynt Creek, 48.
PINDLE (Pingle), Thomas, 17,
41.
Piscataway [settlement], (See
also Indians) 13, 67, 72.
Piscataway River, 78.
Branch of, 34, (main) 52,
64.
Creek, 65, 67.
East side of, 5, 67, 72.
Main Fresh (Run), 43, 54,
65.
"Pitchcraft," 54.
Plaisterer (See Occupation).
Planter (See Occupation).
PLOWDEN, George, 35.
Margrett, 35.

"Plummers Pleasure," 6, 60.
Addition to, 60.
POPE, Henry, 3.
"Poplar Hills," 23, 66.
"Poplar Ridge," 1.
Port Tobacco (Charles
County), 67.
Potomac (Potomack) River,
42, 50.
Above the falls, 5.
East side of, 14.
Eastern Branch [Anacostia],
5, 8, 28, 44, 55, 56, 58,
59, 62, 68.
POTTINGER, John, 75.
POTTS, Hannah (Edwards), 30.
John, 16, 30.
POWELL, William, 2, 49.
PRATER (Prather),
Jonathan, 16.
Thomas, 48, 49.
"Prevention," 22.
PRICE, Edward, 38.
Province (See Maryland).
"Purchase," 22.

"Quick Sale (Quick Saile),"
22, 23, 61.

RAMSAY (Ramsey), John, 7,
46.
RAWLINGS, Aaron, 27.
RAY(E), William, 33, 46.
REALE (See RILEY).
Rebellion, 27.
"Redding," 53.
"Reighleys Lott" (See "Rileys
Lott").
REILEY (See RILEY).
"Reparration (Repairation),"
45.
"Retalliation," 22.
Revolution, 26, 27.
REYLEY (See RILEY).
REYNOLD, Tho., 31.

SMALL, David, 11, 13, 26, 31, 33, 34, 46, 48, 57, 58, 74.
SMITH, Ann, 56, 60.
  Anthony, 10.
  John, 18, 22, 23, 29, 31, 46, 55, 56, 60.
  Mary, 6, 12.
  Nathan, 64, 68.
  Ralph, 27.
  Robert, 27.
  Thomas, 6, 73.
  Maj. Wallter, 62.
  William, 74.
"Smithfield," 34.
"Smiths Choyce," 42.
"Smiths Purchase," 10.
SNELLSON, John, 5.
SOLLARS, Mary, 75.
  Robert, 75.
"Something," 25, 26, 46.
SPICER, George, 32, 55.
SPORNE, Nicho's, 41, 55.
SPRIGG, John, 9, 63.
  Margrett, 62.
  Sarah (Pearce), 63.
  Thomas, 68, 69.
  Thomas Jr., 11, 40, 47, 61, 62, 65, 70, 75, 77.
  Thomas Sr., 45, 63.
SPRY, Elizabeth, 41.
  Francis, 35, 41.
STAFFORD, Thomas, 8.
STALEY, Thomas, 27.
STANLEY, John, 35.
  Robert, 32.
STEPHENS, Richard, 42.
  Sarah, 42.
"Stephens his Hope," 42.
STOCKETT, Thomas, 40, 53, 76, 77.
STODDART (Stoddard, Stoddert), James, 4, 11, 33, 41, 42, 46, 47, 53, 59, 60, 63, 64, 69, 73, 74, 76, 77.
  Mary, 60.

STONE, Theadosia Wade, 36.
  William, 7, 20, 36, 37, 77.
"Stoney Hill" (Also called "Arthers Folly"), 50.
STORTAN, Robert, 9.
STOTT, Thomas, 66.
STRAWBERRY, Charles, 55.
STREET, Francis, 61.
"Strife":
  John Addison's (bounds on Mattawoman Branch), 67.
  Henry Darnall's (on west side of Patuxent River near tract "Dunkell"), 6.
SULLIVAN (Swillivan), Jeremiah, 36.
SUMMERS, John, 9.
Surveyor, 41.
Swan Creek (Also called Jeroms Creek), 67.
SWANTONE, Francis, 6.
"Sway," 45.
SWILLIVAN (See SULLIVAN).
SWINSEN, Francis, 59.
SYK, John, 34.

Tailor (See Occupation).
TAILLOR (See TAYLOR).
TALLBOT (Talburt, Tallbut), John, 43.
  Sarah Locker, 43.
TANDELL, Bridgett (See FENDALL, Bridgett).
TANEY (Tanney, Tawney), Jane, 18.
  Mich., 40.
  Thomas, 18, 24, 77.
TANEYHILL (Tanyhill), William, 42, 46, 60, 62, 67, 71.
TASKER, John, 53.
  Thom's, 27.
TATE, John, 2, 30.
TAWNEY (See TANEY).
TAYLARD, William, 28.

Virginia, (continued)
North'ton County, 16.

WADE, Robert, 5, 6, 11, 15,
    17, 34, 43, 62, 67.
  Theodosia (Stone), 36.
  Zacharia, 36, 37.
WALLKER, Cha., 41.
WARD(E), Murphey, 55, 60.
"Wards Pasture," 60.
"Warmister," 1.
WATTS, Allexander, 10.
WATTSON, William, 67.
"Waughtown (Waughton)," 58.
"Wedge," 19.
WEIGHT (See WIGHTE).
WELLS, Thomas, 6, 27.
WEST, Jno., 14.
Western Branch (See Patuxent
    River).
WHEELER, Dorathy, 72.
  Francis, 12, 13, 38.
  Ignatius, 12, 13.
  Jana., 38.
  John, 42, 52, 72.
"Wheelers Adventure," 42.
"Whelers Purchase," 72.
WHITE, James, 45.
White Chapel (St. Mary's Co.),
    29.
"White Lackington," 44.
WICKHAM, Nathaniel, 46, 49.
"Wickhams Purchase," 49.
"Widdows Purchase," 39, 64.
WIGHT(E), Ann, 35.
  John, 1, 3, 4, 10, 12, 14,
    18, 19, 23, 25, 31, 32,
    35, 67, 69.
WILKINSON (Willkeson),
  William, 3, 4, 45.
WILLET, Edward, 2, 13, 21,
    24, 32, 33, 34, 35, 37,
    38, 40, 46, 48, 49, 55,
    63, 65, 66, 68, 76.
WILLIAMS, Charles, 1, 9, 23,
    53.

WILLIAMS, (continued)
  James, 20, 21, 52.
  Joseph, 70.
  Mary, 21.
  Samuell, 42.
WILSON (Willson, Willsone),
  Alex'r, 24.
  Jonn'n, 14, 20.
  Maj. Josias, 39, 53, (High
    Sheriff) 77.
  Martha Lingan, 53.
  Thomas, 2, 30, 37.
WITTAM, William, 9.
"Wolves Den," 22.
WOOD, Edward, 3, 18.
"Woodbridge," 9.
"Woods Joy," 3, 4, 18.
WYLIS, Will., 26.

"Yarmouth," 59.
"Yarrow (Yarow)," 5, 59.
"Yarrow Head," 59.
YATES (Yatte, Yeats, Yeates),
  George, 1, 45.
  Mary, 1, 9, 23, 35, 53, 76.
YOUNG, George, 64.
  William, 35.

Zaniah [Zekiah] Branch, 12.

www.ingramcontent.com/pod-product-compliance
Lightning Source LLC
Chambersburg PA
CBHW070116300326
41934CB00035B/1376